P  D

INSIDE THE PREACHER'S MIND

BRIAN THOMPSON

A CIP catalogue record for this book is available from the British Library.

ISBN 978-1-7398902-1-6

Book layout and cover design by Clare Brayshaw

Cover image Albrecht Dürer: Praying Hands

Prepared and printed by:

York Publishing Services Ltd
64 Hallfield Road
Layerthorpe
York YO31 7ZQ

Tel: 01904 431213

Website: www.yps-publishing.co.uk

My special thanks to two local preacher friends
for their wisdom and support

Janet Taylor
(Leeds)

Tony Judd
(Knutsford)

CONTENTS

PREFACE

As indicated in my first book, "Sermons in Stones," I really wanted to extend my scope beyond the narrow window of sermons written during lockdown to include the much wider range of sermons preached at other times in a long ministry. This is it and I hope you will find at least some of the inspiration and enthusiasm given to me in their writing and delivery. Of course you will find some sermons where you think I have gone off track theologically. I trust that we can agree to disagree amicably. It seems to be a good biblical principle and I suggest that many churches have a mixture of people with differing views who nevertheless get on together in a spirit of Christian love and fellowship. My sermon on Neighbours covers this.

The title for this book is simply the one given to the first sermon. It could provide an insight into the thought processes preachers have as they start to make their first notes. Where did the initial idea come from, where is the sermon going, is the way ahead clear or is it getting muddled and losing its listeners: are all questions to be pondered and shared – maybe even with the preacher? It is not the preacher's role to simply provide answers. More important is that listeners go away asking questions about God, their faith and what is involved in being a Christian in today's world.

The search for God is lifelong and exciting. "What will I find if I commit myself to Christ?" was put to a Celtic missionary. The reply was "Wonder upon wonder and every one of them true!"

May we discover the truth of that in our lives.

Brian Thompson Knutsford August 2022

INSIDE THE
PREACHER'S MIND

A training course for Methodist Local Preachers required them to write what is known as a Narrative Sermon. What is a narrative sermon? Well it's a posh name for a story. One method would be for the preacher to retell a bible incident as if he or she were actually there when it happened. For instance it could begin with, say:

> "Jerusalem was crowded with pilgrims for the Passover Celebrations. I was in the Temple about to change my money so I could make my special offering when there was a great disturbance. An angry looking man grabbed hold of the money changer's table and tipped it over........"

The whole of the rest of the sermon would then be devoted to how he, as the onlooker, reacted – perhaps by finding out more about this rioter, Jesus, and maybe tracking this travelling rabbi from Nazareth throughout the remainder of that dramatic week. There's plenty of scope for the imagination. I suppose it's the same sort of exercise that writers of historical novels engage in- putting yourself back in time and telling us what you imagine may have happened.

That type of narrative sermon is called a personalised narrative sermon. There is another type called a Parallel Narrative Sermon. This is where the preacher makes up or retells a story, most likely set in modern times, which may or may not have anything to do with religion but where, perhaps in the last sentence even, a parallel is drawn with a bible story or verse. It can be effective. Think of the parable of the Good Samaritan with its telling conclusion: "Go and do thou likewise." The questioner, who had asked simply "Who is my neighbour?" had been told a story and had been given the point – in the punchline.

All preachers bring these story telling skills into parts of their sermons, but to hear a sermon which is all narrative, standing on its own as a complete story, is a rare experience for congregations. Well, stand by, because this morning's effort is about to turn into a narrative sermon. And it will not be too lengthy, though longer than Jesus's parables – but he was, after all, a master story teller and preacher, who often used this method of getting his message across. Stories such as the Prodigal Son and the Good Samaritan come to everyone's mind because they have found a place in the list of the world's greatest stories.

Jesus's stories, or parables, were set in his time, but had a message for all times. They were designed to challenge his listeners – not to give them all the answers but to send them away working out their own conclusions about their relationship with God and with other people, about belief and behaviour. The disciples would talk amongst themselves as to what Jesus meant.

Sometimes they would take him on one side and ask him, "Master, we don't quite understand this. Can you explain it a bit more?" But mostly the parables' messages were uncomfortably clear in terms of rebuke, of demand for change of attitude, and of challenge to action. Jesus looked for the best in his followers (he still does) and that always involves some adjustments and sacrifices. Don't expect to follow Jesus and remain the same!

But for those who make a commitment to Christ there are, of course, stacks of blessings and tons of help. If you sometimes doubt that, then remember the words of Jesus:

"I have come so that you may have life to the full." (John 10v.10)

Then browse through the gospels (especially John) looking for some of the many promises of Jesus which help to turn his overall promise of abundant living into some sort of reality.

So we come to my narrative sermon which is technically a parallel narrative – but you needn't remember that because it's not important. I have given it a title:

"Inside the Preacher's Mind"

Inside the Preacher's Mind

The preacher placed his sermon notes on the pulpit lectern and, having fixed the first sentence in his mind, he surveyed the congregation and waited for the hymn before the sermon to finish. Perhaps he should have been concentrating on the words they were singing – after all he had chosen the hymn with his usual care: but, with a mixture of nervous trepidation and love, his eyes wandered over the heads buried in books.

Some of the gathered assembly he had known for years. He had been privileged to share in their joys and sorrows, and had come to terms with their idiosyncracies, which included the odd irritating feature but many more qualities which he admired and recognised as God given.

He reflected on his own faults though, hoping that others could be as understanding and forgiving as he tried, not always successfully, to be.

He had realised a long time ago that the Christian path was not an easy one to tread – and that being a preacher increased the dangers of pride and hypocrisy. Sometimes he was painfully aware of a gap between preaching and practice. If he couldn't always come to terms with himself how could he hope to get into the hearts and minds of folk who listened to his sermons? Over his years in the pulpit his attempted aim had been to get alongside his hearers, to endeavour to put himself into their shoes, to be like Ezekiel when he said, "I sat where they sat" (the prophet/preacher identifying there with his fellow Jews exiled in Babylon, in shock and mourning for their beloved homeland.)

Like Ezekiel our modern preacher cum prophet was charged with the task of making God real to his listeners in their situation. But unlike Ezekiel's day here was no unifying national crisis. (The coronavirus pandemic was still to come). My audience, (he realised), these people in front of me all have their own individual situations to face when they leave the tranquil, restoring oasis of worship in this special building. "Therein lies my dilemma!" he mused. He quickly corrected himself with a prayer. "Hang on a minute. Forgive me, Lord. It's not my problem! Isn't this where the Holy Spirit comes in?"

He recalled occasions when after a service remarks like "You had a word for me today," had been made to him and he had been humbled because through him, and in spite of him, God had spoken to someone's heart. Preachers never cease to be amazed and thrilled whenever this happens.

(At this point you might be thinking: It's taking a long time to sing the final verse of the hymn. Is the organist on a 'go slow'? But it's like in one of your waking dreams – astonishing how much detail can be packed into a few brief seconds.)

So halfway through that last verse our preacher's eyes rest on a couple near the front who are even older than he is. They have been happily married for many years. They did their courting on the back row of this church. They are now blessed with a large family, which includes great grandchildren. But their happiness is marred by the behaviour of two teenagers in their family who are going off the rails, whose friends binge drink and maybe take drugs. So they have come to church this morning with a great burden of anxiety for certain family members.

Their former spot on the back row is today occupied by a young couple, obviously in love, sitting hand in hand, occasionally looking to the front but frequently gazing into each other's eyes. "Shan't get much of their attention," the preacher smiled, "but not many worshippers will go away as happy as they are! Let's hope they keep God in their future life together, as the man and wife near the front have done."

The preacher also notices, with a pang of sympathy, a middle aged woman recently widowed and still deep in shock. He also sees a young professional husband and wife, trying to meet the demands of their busy careers whilst bringing up two small children. They are grateful for the regular help of grandparents.

Off to one side there is a middle aged pair struggling to maintain their mortgage since the husband was made redundant. In the corner at the back as if trying to hide there sits an unmarried mother with her three year old boy, existing on benefits yet desperate to be able to support herself.

Other small children are present in the church – bright eyed, noisy and full of life. Teenagers too with exam pressures and other challenges, causing the preacher to reflect: "It's harder growing up today than when I was a lad!"

As the preacher's eyes rove he realises what a wide spectrum of people he is about to address:

single, married, widowed, divorced; young, middle aged, older still. (he doesn't like the word 'elderly'); the fit and a few infirm, the comfortably placed and those having all on to make ends meet. There is even a handful of asylum seekers and refugees, missing their home and families and feeling vulnerable in this foreign land.

"Some individuals here are coping with life's problems," he thought, "others are not. Some are fulfilled and happy, looking forward with hope; others are sad, lonely, hurting, depressed. Some are fearful of what the future will bring, even what this week holds for them, or for their loved ones."

"All these people (the preacher mused) have travelled to church this morning by different routes, coming together as one. Yet each person is on her or his peculiar journey through life. No one is exactly alike or at the same stage. "Where else would you find such a mixture, such a hotch-potch, of different human beings?" he wondered. "And what is the mystical, magical element which unites this odd bunch in song and prayer, in listening to words of scripture and in some preacher's fumbling attempts to make sense for them of what it means to live a Christian life in this modern, secular society which often has little time or respect for anything to do with God."

"And to add to all this mixture there are people before me who are at different levels in their faith! Some have been Christians for years, others are barely beginning. Some are still searching, others have grave doubts and misgivings even after years of attending church.

Such a widespread and rich diversity amazingly united in this one act of worship!" he concluded. "And it happens week after week, not just here but all over the world."

The preacher mouthed a silent "Wow!" and then went on to ask himself: "Why should this be?

How can this happen? What is the explanation for this strange phenomenon?"

The truth dawned upon him in a startling flash as he caught sight of a large banner with the words *All one in Christ.* That's the answer! Jesus is the uniting factor! It's all about Jesus!"

"And here am I," he thought with a twinge of inadequacy, "charged with the responsibility of presenting God's word to these folk today, of making Jesus real to them in their homes, schools, workplaces, situations, tomorrow and in the week ahead."

Self doubts crept into his mind: "Maybe it's time to hang up my preaching gown. Over half a century of preaching! That's a lot of words. To what avail?" He pushed these thoughts to one side for later consideration – but remained overawed at the seemingly impossible task that now lay before him as the hymn finished and the congregation sat down ready to listen to what he had to say.

Urgently and silently he prayed: "Please, Lord, I sure need your help! I've done my preparation diligently but it's over to you now to do what you can with my efforts."

And so he began his sermon. It was Pentecost Sunday, with its marvellous set reading from Acts, chapter 2. "Maybe, (he thought), the most important chapter in the whole of the New Testament for not only was the coming of the Holy Spirit being described but this marked the birth of the Church."

It was only on the following day, thinking back, that it occurred to him that his pre-sermon reflections could be summed up in his chosen text: "When the day of Pentecost came the disciples were all together in one place.."

Isn't that what had happened yesterday where he had preached, and at churches everywhere?

The worshipping, servant Church, having grown from small beginnings into a worldwide movement in 20 centuries is still powered by the Holy Spirit and therefore still growing. Had the same Holy Spirit, the same loving Father God, the same living Lord Jesus moved hearts and changed lives in the preacher's congregation?

God knew the answer to that question – he, the preacher, didn't really need to know.

He filed his sermon notes in his sermons drawer and turned his attention to his next preaching appointment. Looking up the lectionary readings he began to wonder what God would want him to say to his next congregation. He discovered that the readings included the first eight verses of Isaiah chapter 6 – the call of Isaiah, as he was worshipping in the Temple, to be a prophet. It was as if God had said "There are people who need to hear my message of love. Who can I send to tell them?" Isaiah replied, "Here am I. Send me."

Most local preachers will tell you that part of their call to preach came within the context of worship. Our preacher began to wonder whether he should challenge his next congregation with the question: "Is God calling *you* to serve him in some way, maybe even as a preacher? Does God say to *you* 'I need helpers'?"

With a blank sheet of paper before him and a pencil in his hand he prayed for some guidance and a lot of inspiration, knowing that God would need some time and a lot of patience to get inside such a butterfly mind!

ADVENT: WAITING IN HOPE

Try to picture a particular scene, a real situation in which I found myself a number of years ago.

It took place at a huge Marks and Spencer shop at the Owlcotes Centre on the boundaries of Leeds and Bradford. The store was crowded. There must have been a sale on – I think It was just before Christmas. I was in the Waiting Area of the Ladies' Changing room. (Gentlemen, nod if this is familiar territory).

There were only a few seats but I squeezed onto the one vacant chair joining 3 or 4 other husbands, patiently waiting for their wives. A lady emerged from the changing room carrying hangers of clothing she had been trying on. She saw us and stopped, fixing us with a surprised gaze and saying in a loud voice, "You do look miserable!" In unison we replied "We are!" A television sketch could not have bettered that moment.

Well here *we* are in another season of Advent trying to unlock the many themes of this busy pre-Christmas period, one of which I suggest is that of WAITING.

Advent has within it threads of Hope, Joy Preparation, Judgement and more for us to unpick and examine – and we have four Sundays to do so before we even arrive at the nativity story of the Christ child lying in a manger.

Four Sundays! So the Early Church Fathers who fixed our Christian calendar must have thought Advent was very important. People today who have little church contact may struggle to work out what the season means, and will be equally at a loss when it comes to Epiphany and more so with Pentecost. In our world of consumerism such seasons have no easy targets for their advertising and marketing skills. We may well be glad of that! Now we are in the waiting of Advent. But this for Christians is different. It is not the anxious waiting that many experience at difficult times in life such as sitting in a dentist's surgery or waiting for exam results or a hospital medical report.

When our younger daughter was at Primary School I used to drive Rachel and a couple of her friends to school on my way to work – three chattery six or seven year old little girls on the back seat. I remember vividly their growing excitement near Christmas and the oft repeated exclamation, "I can't wait for Christmas Day!"

From my own childhood I recall starting a calendar countdown to Christmas with 100 days to go – round about the 15th September.

Strangely enough I did the same thing when I was posted to Egypt straight after my initial training as a young national service soldier.

I still have the shorthand text book where I wrote all the numbers on the blank pages at the back – starting at 593 and going down to number 1 (demob day!) From time to time it was satisfying to cross off a few days. Actually as I buckled down I came to realise that life wasn't so bad after all and I learned a lot, grew up a bit and made many friends. I still looked forward to going home but the waiting was no longer threatening, or soul destroying.

The story goes that all those years ago in Bethlehem two locals were standing at the side of the road. Three camels passed by carrying important looking men.

"Isn't that just typical?" one of the locals said. "You wait for ages then three come together."

There is a bus stop outside my residence in Knutsford. We have a limited car park so whenever I'm expecting visitors I tell them to park on the road at the bus stop – because it's redundant. The bus route has been discontinued.

We won't delve into the local train services! The long promised and long awaited Northern Power House doesn't appear to generate much power. (But I'm not here to spark off any arguments on that issue!)

In our nativity stories we find hints of another sort of power – Divine power, God at work in peoples' lives and in the things that happened. And we can see how that power often involved times of waiting, patience and anticipation.

For instance, travellers from afar, prompted by their study of the stars, detecting an astrological message, had to plan a long journey and buy expensive gifts. That would take time and they couldn't just hop onto a Northern Rail train.

Shepherds, looking after their sheep at night eagerly awaited the safety of dawn when the dangers of attacks from wild animals passed. They didn't hang around though when the angels' message sent them hurrying off to Bethlehem!

Mary and Joseph, more than the others, knew all about waiting, and the unwanted journey to Bethlehem at a critical time must have given them painful lessons in coping with anxiety.

Even Herod the Great is shown as waiting – waiting for the opportunity to exterminate yet another possible rival to his kingly power. He was usually successful but on this occasion he was thwarted – by the wisdom of the Magi and the power of a higher ruler: God.

It's only in Matthew and Luke that we find the birth stories of Jesus and in only four chapters. There are discrepancies between the two accounts and the writers may have embroidered their stories in places but the themes they included, such as waiting, were obviously important to them.

When they set their scenes they refer back to the nation's prophets. We echo them when we sing "Long ago prophets knew Christ would come born a Jew".

As we read the birth stories we get the impression that Jesus was born into a society at a time people were looking for God to rescue them from the harsh domination of their Roman rulers – by sending a Messiah. In spite of their conquered situation they had not lost hope. To quote another great Advent hymn:

"Weary was our heart with waiting,
and the night watch seemed so long;
but his triumph day is breaking
and we hail it with a song.

There's a hush of expectation,
and a quiet in the air; and the breath of God
is moving in the fervent breath of prayer"

So a link has been established between Advent and waiting. At that point in my sermon writing I hit the brick wall. It often happens!

I had the feeling that something was missing. After all there is much more to Advent than just waiting. But I didn't know how to proceed.

A few days later I picked up a book from my bedside table – a book for dipping into before going to sleep. It is a selection of short extracts from the many writings of Walter Brueggemann a renowned American Bible scholar, writer and University professor.

I recommend such bedtime reading. There is nothing like a good bit of theology to send you to sleep – which is why I often split my sermons in two or more parts. I do *not* lay claims to be a preacher of good theology but I *do* try to ensure that my listeners are not given the time to fall asleep.

Brueggemann's book has the simple title: "A Gospel of Hope." Flicking quickly through some of the chapters before falling into bed I came across passages which were to me gems of wisdom and inspiration. I share briefly just a couple:

"Hope ... is not just a vague feeling that things will work out, when it is evident that things will not just work out. Rather, hope is the conviction, against a great deal of data, that God is tenacious and persistent in overcoming the deathliness of this world, that God intends joy and peace. Christians find compelling evidence in the story of Jesus, that Jesus, with great persistence and great vulnerability, everywhere he went, turned the enmity of society toward a new possibility, turned the sadness of the world toward joy, introduced a new regime where the dead are raised, the lost are found, and the displaced are brought home again. We draw our hope from the breathtaking memory of this Jesus!" (p.104)

and elsewhere:

"What a stunning vocation for the church, to stand free and hope-filled in a world gone fearful, and to think, imagine, dream, vision a future that God will yet enact. What a work of visioning for the church, when society all around is paralised in fear, preoccupied by commodity, mesmerised by wealth, seeking endless power, and deeply, deeply frightened. And here is this little community of God-visited people, not greedy, not fearful, not in despair ... dreaming about the way of peace among peoples, visioning about justice between haves and have nots, prophesying about an ordered earth, curbed enough of greed to respect the environment, able to be inclusive of those who are different from us ..."(p.103) Brueggemann concludes: *"Hope is the deep religious conviction that God has not quit."*(105)

Within the Nativity stories provided by the gospels of Matthew and Luke we find not only lots of WAITING but also lots of HOPE. At last I had a sermon title: WAITING IN HOPE.

Earlier we looked at those who waited. It occurs to me that most of these "waiters" were also the "hopers". They included the spiritually alert in the land who, in spite of Roman oppression, had not given up on God and his promise of a Messiah. They knew that God had not quit on them and they would not quit on him. There were the shepherds whose hopes were rekindled by the songs of angels and the sight of a baby lying in a manger. There were those who *travelled* in hope – Mary and Joseph on their long journey from Nazareth to Bethlehem; the Magi or Wise Men on their even longer journey.

In the poem "The Journey of the Magi" by T.S.Eliot one of the magi describes their journey, beginning with the words:

> *"A cold coming we had of it, Just the worst time*
> *of the year for a journey, and such a long journey;*
> *the ways deep and the weather sharp, the very*
> *dead of winter."*

He describes some of the events en route and finishes with this:

> *"All this was a long time ago, I remember.*
> *And I would do it again but set down this,*
> *Set down this: were we led all that way for*
> *For Birth or Death? There was a birth,*
> *Certainly we had evidence and no doubt.*

I had seen birth and death, but had thought
they were different; this birth was hard and
bitter agony for us, like death, our death.
We returned to our places, these Kingdoms,
But no longer at ease here, in the old
dispensation, with an alien people clutching
their gods. I should be glad of another death

This juxtapositioning of birth and death in the nativity stories, was foreseen by the old man Simeon when the baby Jesus was presented in the Temple (Luke 2v25-35). After blessing the baby his words to Mary were "and a sword will pierce your own soul too"

Is there not also a hint of suffering ahead in that gift of myrrh brought by one of Matthew's Wise Men? Myrrh was the ointment used to embalm bodies of the dead. Hardly a suitable gift for a baby just starting out on life!

I remember years ago a Sunday School nativity play we put on at our church in Leeds.

We used a spotlight. As the building darkened. its beam caught a wooden cross on the top of the piano, projecting its shadow across the stable scene. It wasn't planned, but it struck me that the shadow of a wooden cross can always be detected in the wooden manger wherein lay the baby who would come to be called the Saviour of the World. The writers of Matthew and Luke wanted us to see this.

In Luke, when the old man Simeon says to Mary "A sword will pierce your own soul too" our minds are meant to fast forward 33 years to a weeping mother watching her nail pierced son dying on a cross outside Jerusalem's city walls.

All of this brings to my mind a sermon I first read many years ago and with this I will close.

The theologian, Paul Tillich, preached this sermon in the 1950s. He gave it the title "Born in the Grave".

In it he tells of a witness at the Nuremburg War Crime Trials who had lived for a time in hiding with fellow Jews in a Jewish cemetery in Wilna, Poland. This witness wrote poetry and one of his poems was the description of a birth. In a nearby grave a young Jewish woman gave birth to her son. An 80 year old grave digger, wrapped in a shroud, assisted. When the new born child uttered his first cry, the old man prayed:

"Great God, hast thou finally sent the Messiah to us? For who else than the Messiah himself can be born in a grave?"

After three days the poet saw the child sucking his mother's tears because she had no milk for him. There's almost too much despair here for us to cope with.

It's like when we see television pictures of starving, injured, innocent suffering children in the world's disaster zones and we want to avert our eyes – but we mustn't. We need to pray, to maintain our concern, maybe to give and to cling on to the thought that there is always hope when a child is born. The young Jewish mother in the grave lovingly cradled her new born son in her arms smiling at him, whispering her love to him, praying for him – with hope in her heart.

Such hope is a gift from God in every birth. It was there in *your* birth and no one can take it from you because it comes from God and is a gift to *you*, and through you to the world. So you can see how precious you really are!

The grave digger's hopes were real too. They were to be dashed – but they had been real. The child probably survived for only a few days and the mother's grief would have been overwhelming, but she would forever treasure and cherish her initial hope. Surely wherever hope and love are found God can be detected. *No circumstance and no one* can take that away from us. God does not quit and cannot be eliminated.

As Advent continues and Christmas draws closer may we wait in hope remembering that we Christians not only *wait* in hope – we are also *travellers* in hope.

My prayer is that you will travel safely through Advent and Christmas, with God's blessing.

In the name of the Father, The Son, And the Holy Spirit. Amen

(Preached at Alderley Edge Methodist Church 8 December 2019)

LOOKING FOR THE REAL CHRISTMAS

Christmas seems to get earlier every year – driven by consumerism and the desire to get us to buy whatever is for sale. We recognise all that and it's hard to resist. The Christian cards and posters which say "Let's put Christ back into Xmas" make the point for us.

I began to think about a new sermon for Advent & Christmas during the last week in September, aware that some shops were already putting out Christmas goods, and Garden Centres had begun to turn into Christmas grottos, that Santa Clauses would soon be welcomed by the big stores, festive lights were being erected in city streets, and seasonal catalogues were dropping through our letter boxes.

Christmas movies had just begun to appear on our TV screens and I had watched one. I am not addicted to them and I see all their sugary, sentimental flaws but occasionally you find one that is enjoyable. The old classics "It's a Wonderful Life" and "Miracle on 24th Street" had something worthwhile saying – even though there was very little, if anything, about the original Christmas story.

Modern movies in the genre all have familiar themes such as young couples meeting, not liking each other but gradually falling in love. The film I watched came as a welcome relief from the angst and bitterness and monotony of the Brexit situation at the time. The films often have common winter features such as Christmas trees and reindeer. Father Christmases and miracles of some sort are essential ingredients. The films must have happy endings often with the young couple kissing under a star-filled sky with large flakes of snow suddenly starting to gently fall.

Slushy, some would say dismissively, unrealistic, sheer escapism. Well maybe. But what's harmful in that? In a society and a world where arrogance, bombastic opinions and self-seeking power have dominated of late can we not allow injections of gentleness, hope and peace a foothold? Did not the Old Testament prophets temper their judgements with messages of hope from God, with dreams and visions of a better and brighter future for their people? All of which required a huge suspension of belief from the harsh realities which daily pressed down upon them.

Christmas movies may well be a form of escapism and they may take us some way from the accounts in the Gospels of the birth of Jesus – but it is not their purpose anyway to forge any more than a tenuous link between the events at Bethlehem and the stories in the films. These films have messages of love and happiness as do the Gospels but it is up to the Church (to us) to proclaim and explain the messages and implications of the coming of Jesus into our world. To do that perhaps we need to look into the nativity stories more deeply than many people do. Hence my sermon title "Looking for the real Christmas".

Christianity, or the Church, was already up and running before stories of the birth of Jesus appeared. St Mark's gospel – the first of our four to be written – has no nativity story. Neither does John. The birth stories then are confined to just two chapters in Matthew and two in Luke. St Paul, whose preaching and writing *pre-dates* Mark, does not mention any of the Christmas stories familiar to us.

For Paul, the *circumstances* of Jesus's birth were of no consequence. His birth as a descendant of David was acknowledged in Paul's letter to the Romans (1v.3) but as there is no mention of angels, no wise men, no guiding star then Paul must have thought it to be a normal birth. "Sent by God born of a woman" (the apostle wrote to the Galatians (4 v.4-5) The *extraordinary* for Paul was the fact that God, by the power of the Spirit, raised Jesus from the dead – thus setting him apart as the Messiah and giving him his unique identity of the Son of God.

St Paul died around AD64, just prior to Mark's gospel being written. The others came later. As Mark omits any nativity accounts it is safe to argue that to those first Christians the birth of Jesus was not important.

When they were baptised into the faith their simple affirmation was "Jesus is Lord!" It was not until the 4th century creeds that words such as "He was conceived by the Holy Spirit and born of the Virgin Mary" began to be used. The essential belief for those early Christians was that their redemption and forgiveness of sin, their reconciliation with God, were achieved through the crucifixion and the resurrection of Jesus. That gospel message remains unaltered today.

A few years ago I received this Christmas card from a pupil in one of my classes: "This Christmas card is guaranteed to be different from all the other cards you'll receive". That's on the outside. Inside we read "HAPPY EASTER!"

Christmas and Christianity make much more sense when we understand what *Easter* means. Most Christmas shoppers, if they give any thought at all to Jesus, (who after all is the reason for this season), probably think that his birth started the ball rolling, whereas actually his resurrection was the trigger – not his birth. So in that sense the boy who sent this card got it right. The birth of Christianity *was* an Easter event not a Christmas event.

How then did stories of shepherds, wise men and angels come to be written by Matthew and Luke when belief in Christ didn't seem to require them?

Well, probably because the growing realisation that Jesus was special, unique, the Son of God in fact, prompted the desire to know about the life of Jesus before he appeared on the public scene when he submitted himself to baptism by John – which is Mark's starting point.

Popular hero figures today get subjected to the same scrutiny. People want to find out all about their lives *before* they became famous. In that respect Mark's biography of Jesus was incomplete.

That explains why Matthew and Luke dug deeper. It was to satisfy people's natural curiosity – although in fact we are told very little about the childhood and early manhood of Jesus the Messiah. But at least we have been given these precious and wonderful nativity stories. They do, however, present the modern reader with certain difficulties. As Christians we should be able to provide some answers to the questions we could be asked.

A few years ago a Methodist minister wrote these words in a letter to the Methodist Recorder:

> *"In this season when legend, myth and the biblical narrative can seem inextricably woven together, I sometimes present people with the following "useful summary" of the Christmas story: The Bible tells us that the three kings on their camels, led by Caspar, followed the star all the way from Persia in the East to the stable in Bethlehem, where they met the shepherds and saw the baby Jesus, born that very night, surrounded by cattle.*

The minister continues.

> *At first there may be polite nods* (from my listeners). *When I point out that there are no less than ten errors of fact in my summary, jaws can begin to drop."*

Christmas continues to arouse tremendous interest partly because it is *visual* in its presentation. Christmas cards, crib scenes and carols make us *see* Mary, Joseph, the baby Jesus, angels, the donkey, sheep, cattle, finely dressed kings, shepherds, all crowded together in the soft, romantic glow of a warm, sweet smelling, comfortable stable – reminiscent of an advertisement for gas central heating. It's a charming image for young and old alike. But it wasn't and never could be just like that!

To start with, given the details of Matthew's account, the travellers from the east, who have been glamourised into Persian kings, (an unlikely harmony of power and peace!) would not have arrived in Bethlehem until Jesus was at least two years old. The Gospel specifies that the star stopped over a house, not the stable. They have moved on!

What we have in most of our carols, cards and crib scenes is an amalgamation of the two separate nativity accounts – forced into one, despite irreconcilable differences between Matthew's version and Luke's. Each of these two evangelists has his own agenda about Jesus. Matthew writes especially for Jews and is anxious that his readers see Jesus as fulfilling the prophecies of the Messiah found in their scriptures.

So Jesus is presented by Matthew, or whoever wrote that gospel (and it certainly wasn't the disciple Matthew) as their new Moses figure. Thus the baby Jesus, like the baby Moses, escapes death from a cruel massacring king. Like Moses Jesus is taken to Egypt – a baby refugee in a foreign land. Like Moses Jesus would be recognised as a teacher and prophet. His sermon on a mount in Galilee would remind them of the Ten Commandments given on Mount Sinai.

That is Matthew's emphasis for his Jewish readers. Luke's audience is wider and he wants his *gentile* readers to know that Jesus is the Son of God and Saviour of all people. If they are lost they will be found. If they are downtrodden they will be raised. If they are humble they will be exalted. Loved by God, they too are heirs of a promised land and they too will feast with God in paradise.

In Matthew's nativity stories Joseph's experiences predominate – his reluctance to marry Mary when he learns that she is pregnant and his guidance from God through dreams.

Luke, on the other hand, lets us see things through Mary's eyes – her acceptance of the Angel Gabriel's startling news, and her visit to her relative Elizabeth, who is the mother to be of John the Baptist.

Matthew tells us of wise men following a moving star, of Herod slaughtering innocent children and of the Holy Family's escape to Egypt. There is none of that in Luke but it's only in Luke that we have a choir of angels telling shepherds not to be afraid. Luke alone records the Roman census causing Mary and Joseph to journey from their home in Nazareth to faraway Bethlehem. It's only in Luke that Anna and Simeon offer worship to baby Jesus in the Temple.

Two different accounts then, raising questions such as: Why is there no record elsewhere of the "worldwide census when Quirinus was governor of Syria"? Why doesn't Matthew mention it?

Wouldn't this forced movement of such vast numbers of people be not only impracticable but also unnecessary – a bureaucratic nightmare in fact. (Quirinus was not governor of Syria anyway until ten years after Herod died)

Then we have the dilemma of the moving star – like an ancient satnav, (minus the irritating voice) conveniently directing the travelling wise men on their journey and then pinpointing the house (note, not a stable!) where the family now lived.

It seems strange too that there is no record outside the New Testament of the resulting massacre of innocent children. The ancient historian, Josephus, tells us a lot about Herod the Great. Surely he would have noted such a barbaric act!

So there are lots of issues for us to grapple with in these nativity stories! We have to realise that Matthew and Luke were not writing pure history. They were presenting important underlying truths about Jesus, and they embroidered the historical bits. They weren't lying – they were bringing out deeper understandings of who Jesus was. They were giving their readers and us information about this unique human being.

In only three areas do we find complete agreement between Matthew and Luke: 1. That Jesus was conceived by the Holy Spirit – a virgin birth we inaccurately call it; the birth was normal, it was the conception that was unique. 2. That Jesus was born in Bethlehem. 3. That he is our Saviour.

These common elements of agreement are really saying that here we have a miraculous birth initiated by God himself. The various stories which both writers found and included are less important than the truth they encapsulate.

This truth is what Christians call THE INCARNATION.

John, the writer of the fourth and last Gospel, proclaims the Incarnation stirringly: "The Word became flesh and dwelt among us, full of grace and truth; we have been shown his glory, glory of the only Son from the Father." (1.14)

Charles Wesley trumpeted the Incarnation with the memorable line expressing his sheer amazement: "Our God contracted to a span, incomprehensibly made man" (STF208) And elsewhere (STF 199): "Jesus is our brother now, and God is all our own."

The Incarnation – that God was in Jesus dwelling among us to bring us back to him – is the important thing to believe.

So it is not a betrayal to have some doubts – about a moving star, wise men bearing expensive gifts, an improbable census, Herod's cruel act – or even the virgin birth – as long as we believe that, in Jesus, God somehow became one of us.

I don't know where you stand on the questions I have raised about the nativity stories, but I'm with the poet, John Betjeman, whose poem "Christmas" includes the lines:

"And is it true? And is it true, This most tremendous tale of all, Seen in a stained glass window's hue, A baby in an ox's stall? The maker of the stars and sea Become a child on earth for me? ....God was man in Palestine, and lives today in bread and wine."

I believe it is true, even though, as you can see, I put question marks against the historical accuracy of some of the details given by Matthew and Luke.

Whether they happened or not though doesn't trouble me because I discover within them certain deeper truths which the writers were seeking to convey about Jesus.

Here are some of them for you to think about. For ease of memory they all start with the letter M.

We have in these stories a contrast between MIGHT and MEEKNESS – the might of Herod and the Romans and the meekness of the Christ child and his parents.

We have MIRTH – seen in the infectious joy and praise of Luke's choir of angels, making the shepherds race off to Bethlehem to see for themselves. One of our Christmas carols speaks of: "News of great joy, news of great mirth" and goes on to ask, "Then why should we on on earth be so sad since our Redeemer makes us glad?"

Gloomy Christians are a contradiction in terms. We follow not just a "Man of Sorrows" – Jesus was more than that. He was, and is, supremely a "Man of Joy." So, cheer up!

Two more M's in these stories are MAGIC and MYSTERY; Not magic in a Harry Potter sense but that which makes us sing of a "Great and Mighty Wonder" (HP90)

The word "wonder" implies mystery. Here indeed is something "incomprehensible." Just because we cannot explain a mystery though doesn't mean it's false. Albert Einstein, once said: "The most beautiful thing we can experience is the mysterious. It is the source of all true art and science."

As well as magic and mystery there is perhaps also an element of MELANCHOLY. Touches of sadness and grief are to be found around that manger. There is a tendency for us to eradicate the dark bits of the story. and a danger of us seeing only a warm, comfortable stable with golden straw, lavish presents and haloes galore.

Luke hints at the pain to come when he has Simeon blessing the baby Jesus in the Temple, and predicting to Mary: "This child will be a sign from God which many will speak against. And sorrow, like a sharp sword will break your own heart." (2v34-5)

I came across a Christmas reading which I want to share with you in closing:

"It's Christmas time at our house and we're putting up a tree. I'd like to find some simple way to mark God's love for me. Some little sign or symbol to show friends stopping by: The little babe was born one day but he really came to die.

Some symbol of his nail pierced hands, the blood he shed for me. What if I hung a nail upon my Christmas tree? I know it was his love for us that held him to a tree, And when I see this simple nail I'll know he died for me. It may seem strange at Christmas time to think of nails and wood, But both were used in Jesus' life to bring us something good. From manger bed, to crown of thorns, to death on Calvary, God used the wood and nails of men to set all people free."

Might, meekness, mirth, magic, mystery and melancholy – they are all there in the nativity stories, thanks to Matthew and Luke. All these M's (and I add three more) help us to see MEANING for our lives, they send out a MESSAGE for the world and they give us, as followers of Jesus, a MISSION to proclaim – the gospel of Good News for all the earth, as our final hymn will remind us. "We have a Gospel to proclaim"

(Preached at St Mark's Swinnow, Leeds 13 on Advent Sunday 2015}

LET'S GO TO GOLGOTHA

The Gospels tell us in some detail, both graphic and gruesome, that Jesus was led away carrying his cross to a hill called Golgotha where he was crucified in a typically brutal Roman public execution.

A number of years ago the Sunday Times organised a short story competition in the Science Fiction genre. It was won with a tale which had the intriguing title "Let's go to Golgotha." The setting was in the far future when a lot of the earth had been built upon and fully explored and even space travel had become dull and boring. A family of man and wife and two small children were faced with the annual problem of "Where shall we go for our annual holiday this year?"

Somewhere different, somewhere exciting was needed but they'd been to most places. In desperation the parents called in at the local travel agent. An obliging fellow, he suggested that they could try a journey in time. He produced various brochures. Why not go back to see the Coronation of Elizabeth I, or perhaps the building of the Pyramids and Sphynx at Giza, Moses leading the Israelites across the Red Sea, maybe a trip to witness the Battle of Waterloo? Eventually they chose their tour. "Let's go to Golgotha, to the crucifixion of Jesus", the parents being persuaded that it would be good for the children's education.

There were, of course, lots of preparations including a lecture from a clergyman who told them, "We will arrive in Jerusalem on the day that Pilate asks the people there who he should set free as the citizens were allowed to grant amnesty to one prisoner over the Feast of Passover."(How generous were the Roman overlords!). The vicar continues: "When the crowd begins to shout 'Barabbas' as you know it will, then you must shout it too. You must not appear to be different in any way from the locals. This is vitally important. You have to appear to be in agreement with the rest of the crowd."

Other sessions follow in treatment rooms where their appearance in dress and facial features is made to match first century dwellers in Jerusalem. They are also given an injection of the local language, which will last for the days of their stay only. It is essential that they merge in with the crowd, for if they are seen as total strangers their lives will be in danger. They are told they must shout out with everyone else for the release of Barabbas and the death of Jesus. They must jeer at Jesus and shake their fists at him as he drags his cross through the street – along the now named Way of the Cross.

Their arrival is exciting but hectic with so many people packing the route to Golgotha. In all the noise and the heat one of the children is feeling ill and so her parents leave the busy thoroughfare looking for shade and somewhere for their daughter to rest. Something strikes them as very odd. Peering into house after house they discover that most of the local people are at home, sitting quietly. After a while they head for the hill of Golgotha. It is too crowded to get near but Jesus is already on the cross. They just manage to catch his words, "Father forgive them; they don't realise what they are doing." Then it dawned on them, the horror of what was happening before their eyes.

Turning to their friends the father shouts "Look at the crowd! Look around you! There are no Jews here, no natives! The only ones here are the time travelling holiday makers. Do you realise the enormity of what we've done? The whole guilt of mankind rests on our shoulders. And we'll do the same next year, and the year after, ad infinitum!"

* * *

We would not want to travel back to see this appalling crucifixion would we – even if it were possible? But in some senses we are still involved, all of us, because the hatred and cruelty and all the sins which helped to crucify Jesus are still around today, in spite of this good man's courage, his love, example and teaching.

People have not listened to Jesus, or do not understand his message of grace and forgiveness. But Christians do, so whenever we hear the story of the crucifixion, or sing about it in our hymns, let us take on board that in his death Jesus was, and is, somehow saying to each one of us:

"See how much I love you!"

Hymns are helpful when they enable us to accept the truth of their words and where we can say "Yes! I agree with that!" From many on the theme of the cross I suggest just two which I find useful and which may help you in your devotions. One is old and one is modern:

That old negro spiritual, "Were you there when they crucified my Lord? Were you there when they crucified my Lord? Oh! Sometimes it causes me to tremble, tremble, tremble. "Were you there when they crucified my Lord?"

That's the *tragedy* side of the cross – and in a way we were there. But be sure to read on to the last verse, "Were you there when God raised him from the dead?" There is the *triumph* aspect – the victory achieved on the cross and in the resurrection – for him and for us to share in.

The other hymn is by Stuart Townend and Keith Getty "How deep the Father's love for us." It has been suggested that maybe Stuart Townend had read Gary Kilworth's science fiction story for his second verse reads:

"Behold the Man upon a cross,
My sin upon his shoulders.
Ashamed, I hear my mocking voice
Call out among the scoffers.
It was my sin that held him there

Until it was accomplished;
His dying breath has brought me life.
I know that it is finished."

Another contemporary hymn makes us pause for thought. The author is Brian Wren and it begins with these words:

"Here hangs a man discarded, a scarecrow hoisted high, a nonsense pointing nowhere to all who hurry by."

In our Scifi story the crowd was rooted to the spot. No hurrying by for them! This scene was after all the point of their time travel holiday. They wanted their full money's worth! But 2000 or so years ago the crowd would not have been as large and would not have had the desire or the stamina to linger for several hours before Jesus uttered his strange words about forgiveness.

A Roman crucifixion was a lengthy and tedious ritual. Many onlookers would soon leave, sick to the guts by this appalling treatment of one of their fellow Jews.

Some indeed would hurry by hardly bearing to look. And many who did cast even a glimpse of Jesus would think like the hymn writer, "What a fool! What a clown of sorrows! Surely he could have avoided this ignominious ending? Madness! Foolish! He had the power to lead a revolt against Rome, to be a Messiah for the Jews and he has thrown it all away!"

We are now well into the season of Lent and our journey towards Good Friday and Easter makes us concentrate a bit more closely on the Cross, and what it means for today. I should finish the Brian Wren hymn verse which I cut short of the question it asks:

"Can such a clown of sorrows
Still bring a useful word,
When faith and love seem phantoms
And every hope absurd?"

And if we cannot say "YES" to that – yes Christ can bring a useful, vital message to today's world then what are we doing here this morning, and what's the point of coming to church at all if we have no hope to bring, no comfort and help to offer, no meaning to point others to, no light for their darkness? Good hymn Brian Wren. Read it again and be encouraged!

So what does the cross say to us? Amongst many things what message can we take away this morning? I share with you two powerful elements which strike me:

The cross is for us and for humankind both a TRAGEDY and also a TRIUMPH. Let's unpick them both.

I read somewhere about a small girl being taken to a church service for the first time. The gospel reading was one of the accounts of Jesus's crucifixion. At the end of the service, as they were leaving, her mother noticed that tears were streaming down her daughter's cheeks.

"Why did they kill him?" the child sobbed.

And why is nobody else crying?" The continuation of the story was apparently not known to her, but for us the question remains – why doesn't the crucifixion of Jesus disturb and upset us more than it does?

I watch an appeal for the NSPCC on the telly and I could cry; I see pictures of starving children and dying women in bombed towns in Syria or in Sudan's refugee camps and choke back the tears; I read a novel or watch a film portraying deep sorrow and loss and find myself welling up, (even during *Call the Midwife!*)

Yet I can read or hear the story of the brutal treatment and ugly death of the One alone whom I am happy to claim, "He is my Friend and my Saviour," and I find myself comparatively unmoved. Why should this be when I love Jesus and I know even more surely that he loves me? Is it because I have heard the story so many times that familiarity has bred, not contempt, but a measure of indifference? Is it because I already know that Easter Day follows Good Friday and there is a gloriously happy ending? Is it because it all happened so long ago that it has lost its immediacy and has become just one more tragic event in a whole quagmire of terrible suffering and wrongs which humanity has inflicted on innocent victims down the centuries?

Or is it because maybe my walk with God is not as close to him as it used to be and I sometimes echo the hymn writer's words:

"Where is the blessedness I knew when first I saw the Lord?" ("O for a closer walk with God")

These questions I have to ask of myself. Do you? Perhaps we need to look again and keep reminding ourselves of the significance of the cross, trying to understand something of what it meant for Jesus then and what it means for us now, and for the world – though of course we shall never fully plumb the depths of this act of divine love.

During the season of Lent many churches, across the denominations, have adopted the custom of transforming a cross. The whole process is poignant and full of meaning.

The cross is sometimes made from the previous year's Christmas tree and stands in a prominent position at the front of the church. On each of the six Sundays in Lent a symbolic reminder of the objects which played a part in the crucifixion is placed by the tree. First 30 silver coins calling to mind the betrayal of Jesus, then a cup for the Last Supper, next a whip for the scourging, then a purple cloak, followed by a crown of thorns and finally three large nails.

Step by step the relentless and dramatic path to the cross is traced and we are made to feel the tension building up for Jesus and his disciples. We try to imagine ourselves actually present during that time.

Then comes Easter Sunday morning and we enter the church to find that somebody has been busy and the bare wooden cross is filled with spring flowers transforming it from an object of ugliness and shame into something beautiful. So we rejoice that our Lord has conquered death and the grave, bringing to the world new life, hope and possibilities of a fresh loveliness.

The whole ceremony of the Lenten Cross is one which I value, but I have to admit that there is a part of it which troubles me and which I have not yet resolved. The question I have is this:

Can we ever transform the cross into something beautiful? Must it not remain what it was at the time – and will always be – an instrument of execution? (with the added deterrent of public humiliation)

Nothing beautiful about that, especially if the crucified one is blameless and a victim of jealousy, hatred and injustice. *Jesus was transformed,* not the cross, which was probably used again, and again and yet again.

And it is *lives that can be transformed* when people come to realise something of what Jesus accomplished for them on the cross: that in some inexplicable way he suffered and died for them, for their sins, to bring them forgiveness, and God's friendship eternally. (and, praise God, the *them* includes *you* and *me*).

The cross was not transformed, but we will always adorn our churches with splendid crosses because the cross has become a powerful symbol of Christianity. Some would say that the cross is at the *centre* of our faith, but doesn't that statement switch the emphasis away from the crucified Lord?

Jesus is at the heart of our faith, not the cross upon which he died! Indeed the Apostle Paul himself, writing to the Corinthians claims that he has been sent to proclaim the Good News of the gospel and to make sure that Christ's death on the cross is not robbed of its power. (1 Cor 1v.23). We preach a crucified Lord.

Many churches prefer a cross without the dying or dead body of our Lord pinned to it because, as the hymn says:

"Christ is alive! Let Christians sing;
His cross stands empty to the sky."

Wearing an empty cross on a gold chain round the neck can be a witness leading into conversation, as some of you will testify, but there must be many non Christians who see it just as a piece of jewellery, without thinking about its significance.

If you don't know who and what it stands for then you might just as well wear a set of hangman's gallows or an electric chair round your neck!

Whilst we must ever recognise the tragedy of the cross we must also never cease to rejoice in the triumph of the cross, and that's the other point I want to make.

That triumph is perfectly illustrated in the prayer we used to start our service. Actually it's the church collect for Passion Sunday, the week before Palm Sunday. I remind you of the relevant bit:

"Most merciful God, who by the death and resurrection of your Son Jesus Christ delivered and saved the world:

grant that by faith in him who suffered on the
cross, we may triumph in the power of his victory;

For the mother of Jesus, and the handful of loyal friends gathered round the cross watching the writhing body of Jesus and trying to catch his every last word as he slowly and painfully slipped away from them the tragedy of all this must have broken their hearts. Neither could the frightened disciples who had turned and fled escape the inconsolable grief of what had happened.

Even on the Sunday morning, a couple of days later, Mary Magdalene in the garden at the tomb, is still crying. "Why are you weeping?" the angels ask her. Moments later the risen Jesus repeats the question, "Why are you weeping?"

Through her tears she has mistaken him for the gardener.

"Mary!" says Jesus – and the seemingly impossible truth begins to dawn! Jesus has come back to life! How can this be? Mary saw Jesus die and that crushing memory, with all the heartbreak it brought, was burned deeply into her whole being.

Could it be that now the time for grieving has gone because out of the tragedy of the cross has come the triumph of resurrection from the grave?

Don't let us confine triumph to the resurrection though because triumphs had already been won on the cross itself.

"It is finished!" Jesus had cried out before he died – in the sense of "It is accomplished; it is done!" Such a shout of triumph suggests that his victories were won on the cross, and sealed by God three days later when he raised him from death. The ultimate victory over the grave!

Somehow or other, known to God alone, but guessed at by scholars and theologians and preachers ever since Jesus died, God turned the tragedy of the cross into a victory, and the triumph of the cross is far greater than its tragedy could ever be – though both remain.

Which is why, of all the world's great religions, Christianity alone has an instrument of execution as its symbol, for in the suffering, dying Jesus we see a number of triumphs:

the victory of love over hatred,
of good over evil, of gentleness over anger,
of courage over cowardice,
of self sacrifice over self preservation.

Whilst we must always recognise the *tragedy* of the cross we must also never cease to rejoice in the *triumphs* of the cross.

Shall I tell you the really good news though? The really good news is that they are triumphs freely given by God to all of us, including you and me, for us to accept, savour and enjoy.

They tell us that God loves us personally, that Jesus died for us, that he wants us to turn to him so that he can welcome and forgive us, and so that we can share all his wonderful goodness – today, tomorrow, next week, next month, the rest of our lives and beyond.

"Life in all its abundance," is how Jesus described it" Wow!

I finish with a meditation, written for Easter Day, and linking the agonies of the cross with suffering humanity today. In some respects the world has not changed but the resurrection does bring great possibilities which we have the duty to proclaim.

The cross stands empty today!
On Good Friday it was the place of torture,
of torment, and of agony:
The place which mirrors so much of life,
life which contains suffering and sorrow for
countless numbers,
throughout history, throughout today.

The cross stands empty today!
On Good Friday it was the place of
embarrassment, of humiliation and defeat;
the place that mirrors so much of life,
life which contains the resignation
and broken spirits of countless numbers,
throughout history, throughout today.

The cross stands empty today!
For Christ is risen from the dead!
Christ is risen from the place of torture,
the place of torment and of agony,
the place of suffering and sorrow;

Christ is risen from the place of embarrassment,
the place of humiliation and defeat,
the place of resignation and broken spirits.
Christ is risen! The cross stands empty today –
BUT THE CROSS REMAINS.

For it is the cross – not any empty tomb, not a discarded shroud, but the cross – which is our symbol and badge for ever.

Resurrection does not rid the world of a cross. Resurrection is God's eternal "YES" to Jesus.

All he said, all he did, all he was, and all that he suffered, now is for ever.

God's Eternal Word!
God's Eternal Life!
God's Redeeming Love!
Our Resurrection Glory
In the sign of an empty cross!

(David Blanchflower. All Year Round Prayers 1993)

(Preached in the Leeds West Circuit. Intended for Plumley Methodist on 15th March 2020 but cancelled by covid.)

EVERYBODY NEEDS
GOOD NEIGHBOURS

To begin with I need to make a confession (and that's got everybody listening.) I have to confess that occasionally, well every weekday actually, I make a habit of watching on the telly (wait for it) NEIGHBOURS.

My excuse is that it all started many years ago when, as a young teacher in a comprehensive school, I was trying to get into the minds of my teenage charges who were all avid fans of this Australian soap. Now I know that it can be a rubbishy series: the acting is often mediocre, the plots are thin and predictable and the stories have little connection with events in the real world. Some stories are too drawn out, whilst at other times, if you miss a few episodes you are left wondering who all the new characters are and whatever happened to so and so. Ramsay Street of Neighbours is untypical of wherever *we* live. *We* don't have an endless stream of *new* neighbours, infidelities, murders, warring families, people in hospital or in prison, or on the verge of a nervous breakdown.

Perhaps the title ought to end with a question mark: "Neighbours?" because it has more than its fair share of bickering. The signature song used to contain the words "Just a friendly wave each morning." Maybe it should have added "and a slap across the face each night!" But I cannot fault the song's statement:

"Neighbours; everybody needs good neighbours." And, after many years, I still watch it!! How pathetic am I? But it could be worse. I could be an avid watcher of "East Enders" or "Hollyoaks!" I wonder how many of you I have offended with that comment? So with a quick "sorry," I'd better move on. We all have our little idiosyncracies. Maybe you think that mine should be called an *idiot*syncrasy! I want to suggest though that in a way "Neighbours, everybody needs good neighbours" is one of the dominant themes of the Bible.

Some Bible scholar described the Old Testament as "the world's great international book," with a message not just for Jews but for ALL people of *every* country and continent. It proclaims, he said, two great truths – The Fatherhood of God and the Brotherhood of Man. Trying to transcribe that description into modern, politically correct terms (as we must), could equate to Parenthood of God and Family of the Human Race -but that loses its punch.

Whatever we choose though we can still affirm our beliefs that God is the Creator of this world and all living things, and that *all* human beings belong to one family. We are brothers and sisters in God's global family, and because God loves us all equally, and without exception, we are obligated to love one another. It is a family privilege and responsibility which God places upon us. It is part of the deal – or of the Covenant as we call it.

We need to clear up one or two popular misconceptions about the Old Testament. Some people see it as a book full of vengeance, portraying God as a cruel and violent tyrant who encourages war, and the merciless slaughter of enemies, even innocent women and children. Today *we* would call that ethnic cleansing. An eye for an eye and a tooth for a tooth, stoning for the blasphemer and adulterer, death for a disobedient son, execution for the homosexual – it's all there (and more) in the books of Leviticus, Deuteronomy, Joshua, Kings, Chronicles and in some of the Psalms. Then, of course there was the complicated and abhorrent practice of animal sacrifice and we are left with the impression of a petulant and punishing God in constant need of being appeased, and being obeyed – a far removal from the picture of a tender, loving, merciful heavenly Father painted for us by Jesus.

This portrayal of a vengeful God is no longer acceptable and we don't have to take it on board. Thankfully most Christians now reject it. We can only begin to understand it a little when we recognise that those ancient people thought of God in that way. To them he was one God amongst many tribal gods, but he was *their* God and he was superior and more powerful than all the others, and it was their duty to be obedient and loyal in order to preserve his, (*and their*), uniqueness amongst the surrounding nations, especially the powerful empires who were a constant threat.

The Israelites' attitude of superiority put them in a dangerous position – it always does. History proves that. To believe that you (or your god) is superior creates within you a divisiveness because you begin to categorise people into "Us" (with a capital U) and "them" (with a small t).

They are inferior, and therefore they can easily be seen as our enemies.

Maybe we see disturbing elements in the Old Testament – but if we look more deeply, and with understanding, we discover glimpses of hope, pearls of great value and insight as the prophets and thinkers began to amend their earlier views of God, and slowly a clearer picture of his nature and his love for *all* nations and each and every person began to emerge. They were commanded, for instance, to "Love your neighbour as yourself" (Lev 19v18). Aliens (i.e. foreigners) were to be treated with respect: thus, Leviticus again: "The foreigner who resides amongst you shall be treated as one of your citizens. You shall love the foreigner as yourself" (Lev 19v34). Some present day right wing groups and individuals still have a long way to go.

Likewise the Israelites had a duty of care to the poor, the widows and the fatherless. Hence the harvest time injunction that parts of the crops were to be left at the edges of the fields for the poor to collect free of charge.

This practice of gleaning is so beautifully seen in the book of Ruth. It was an early food bank!

Ruth herself was a foreigner, but worthy of praise because her great grandson was no less than the greatest of Israel's monarchs – King David.

The comic strip story of Jonah is another Bible book which clearly shows God's love for all people – even the unruly Ninevites, whom the reluctant prophet found impossible to like. Elsewhere within the ancient Hebrew scriptures we find plenty of evidence that God loves *all* the nations, not just the Jews. Did not their esteemed prophet Isaiah remind them in their exile in Babylon that they were specially chosen to be "a light to the Gentiles" (42v.6)? They were given a mission – not to keep God to themselves, but to share him with the whole world.

So the Old Testament can rightly be called the world's great international book. And the New Testament continues those twin themes of the Fatherhood of God and the Brotherhood of Man as it turns the spotlight on what Jesus did and said – and in what happened to him.

Where do we begin in the New Testament – and where do we end? There is so much material in the Gospels (and in the picture of the emerging church given in the Acts and the Letters), to highlight and underline the suggestion that we are neighbours in God's family – and that everybody needs good neighbours. But what will come to all of our minds is that now world famous story in Luke, chapter 10. Jesus had been asked "What must I do to inherit eternal life?" The reply given to the earnest enquirer was in the form of another question.

(Jesus was like that. He didn't just give straight answers. He made people do their own thinking. He still does!)

"What does the Law (the scriptures) say?" The right answer comes back: "You shall love the Lord your God with all your heart, soul, mind and strength; and love your neighbour as yourself." You can almost feel Jesus's, "Well done!" But the questioner is not quite satisfied. "Who *is* my neighbour?" he responds, which leads, of course, to the parable of the Good Samaritan.

On another occasion Jesus was tested by a group of Pharisees who asked him what was the greatest of the 613 commandments in their scriptures. They were told that the greatest is to love God with all our heart and soul.

Then Jesus pointed out that this love for God leads to the consequent and equally important command to love our neighbours as we love ourselves. "On these two commandments," he concluded, "hang all the Law and all the Prophets." (Matthew 22) The implication is that you cannot have the first (loving God) without the second (loving your neighbour).

We can see why James, in his short letter placed towards the end of the New Testament, refers to loving your neighbours as "the royal Law of the Scriptures," and why he places so much emphasis on a Christian's love *in action*. Faith without corresponding works is dead. The world still sees, *and sees through,* those from all faiths (and none) who claim to be religious (or just good) but who ignore the needs of others, those who in the name of religion (but not in its true spirit) commit cruel and inhuman acts, those who seem more intent on revenge rather than mercy, those whose "religion" is judgmental, exclusive and a million miles from the all embracing loving example of Jesus. The hypocrisy is recognised. We are not deceived.

There is a remarkable verse in the book of Malachi, at the end of the Old Testament (1v11) The prophet puts these words into the mouth of God: "From the rising of the sun to its setting my name is great among the nations, and in *every* place incense is offered *to my name*, and it is a pure offering.." Malachi seems to be saying that *all* genuine worship is accepted by God whether or not the worshippers had the same conception of God as did faithful Jews.

Now, by extension, in our 21st century terms the Hindus in their temples, the Jews in their synagogues, the Sikhs in their gurdwaras, the Muslims in their mosques and Christians in churches are all children of one Father God and he accepts the prayers of his children, no matter what label they wear. It's the sincerity of the worshippers that counts. Thank God that he has made himself known to you in Jesus but do not deny that he reveals himself in other Faiths. The Holy Spirit came upon the disciples at Pentecost, but the Spirit of God is surely not confined to Christianity! It is after all by accident of birth that most of us of us here began life in a western Christian-rooted country. I like to think that had I been born elsewhere, I might have become a sincere God-seeking Hindu, Jew, Muslim or whatever.

Since moving to Knutsford from Yorkshire last December I have been greatly encouraged by the warm welcome I have been given especially from members at Knutsford Methodist Church. I am frequently asked "How are you settling?"

And very occasionally "What are you missing about Leeds?"

Well, I miss my local church there, which is a small ecumenical partnership of Methodists, Baptists and United Reform coming together into a new building in the late 1980s and I treasure all the exciting things we learned and did in those early years. I miss seeing my church friends of course and the men at our Leeds Methodist Luncheon Club. I miss the splendid Wesley Singers Choir wonderfully led by Barry and Pat Jordan. Also I miss my Muslim neighbours across the road whose weddings and funerals we have shared over the years and whose help I could call upon at any time of the day or night. I have been a guest at their annual end of Ramadan party for the last three years and have a warm invitation to continue to travel to that Eid ul Fitr celebration where all their extended family of about fifty will treat me and any guests I'd like to take, as royalty – and they would send us home with even more food.

The Leeds interfaith group called Concorde, is an organisation I have come to value. We have explored our beliefs and practices and places of worship in monthly meetings and worshipped together in an annual Civic Peace Service. Each year also we have walked together in a Saturday "Walk of Friendship" through the streets, going into different worship places and often being given a free lunch. (The Sikhs, with their weekly langar open to all, was always the best!) The Walk itself and the banners carried proclaim that there is one God, one world and one family of humankind. I miss all that.

Sadly recent events in New Zealand, and copied elsewhere, along with the hate campaigns of some groups and even some aspects of Brexit publicity have tended to divide and stir up fears over immigration and foreigners – making us into a fragmented and divided nation.

A distinguished 20th century Roman Catholic theologian, Hans Kung, wrote that there can be no peace in the world until the great religions of the world learn to live together in harmony and work together in love. So what can *we* do as individuals? I believe that God calls all of his children to walk in friendship with him. For Christians our walk with God is through Jesus. Each day let us enjoy his surprising companionship and constant love, thanking him for our fellow Christian travellers on the road with us. Often God has opened our eyes to new truths and our lives to fresh experiences. Let's be prepared to extend the hand of friendship not just across denominational divides, but also to those who worship the same one God in ways determined by their different countries of birth and their different cultural upbringing.

A popular American preacher and writer, Brian McLaren, recently wrote a book about Christian identity in our multi-faith world. It has the intriguing title,

"Why did Jesus, Moses, The Buddha and Muhammad Cross the Road?" The answer, he suggests, is not to get to the other side, but to walk alongside each other in friendship, setting the example for followers of all faiths to really get to know one another – in fact to become neighbours and friends working together in love and harmony for the peace of the whole world.

The 19th century saw the spread of Christian missions across the globe. The 20th century brought the separated churches together through the Ecumenical Movement. Maybe the challenge for the World Church in this 21st century lies in the interfaith arena. That begins on each individual church's doorstep – in other words with you, and me, because we live in a multi-faith, multi-cultural country. Maybe you are rightly thinking that in this part of Cheshire we don't get many opportunities to extend the hand of friendship to people of other faiths. Fair enough – but we can still try to learn about ways which differ from ours and we can still come to acknowledge what *unites* the world religions and we can still respect others as neighbours, without trying to impose our views or convert.

Perhaps one day I'll quit watching television's *Neighbours* but I hope I shall never reject my firm conviction that

"Neighbours? Everybody needs good neighbours."

(Preached at Knutsford Methodist Church on 14th July 2019. An earlier version was preached at a Home Missions service at Garforth, North Leeds on 4th October 2015)

SEARCHING FOR GOD

"You don't hear many sermons about God these days." So said a distinguished preacher at a conference on worship. Is that true, I wonder?

We hear plenty of sermons about the Church, and about the life and teaching of Jesus. There is much instruction on faith and prayer, lots of reminders of Christian duties. Frequently we hear what is wrong with our world and our society and we are challenged to some sort of Christian response.

The Church's calendar keeps us in touch with the important festivals and the church lectionary is designed to make certain that we receive systematic and regular instruction from God's Word to us in the Bible. *All that* adds up to a very comprehensive programme of preaching.

The speaker was asking us to consider whether, in all this wealth of sermon material, it could be possible for God to get sidelined. There are so many trees that we miss the wood, as it were. He suggested that although we hear sermon after sermon exploring what it means to *believe* in God, rarely is preaching time spent on God himself.

Questions such as, "What do we mean when we use the word God? Who is God? What is God like? What does God do? How can we know God?" are on the whole left to students of Religious Philosophy and not covered from the pulpit. Maybe there is an assumption that we already know a lot about God, but how well could we put our "knowledge" of God into words? Could you give a satisfactory answer to someone who asked you, "Will you tell me about this God that you claim to worship?"

I guess that all of us would probably find some difficulty with a question like that – and it's hardly surprising because the whole concept of God is not easy. In fact God is somewhat of a problem! How do we set about defining God?

It would be different if God were a physical reality like, say, Mrs Jones who lives around the corner. We know a lot about Mrs Jones because we often meet and chat to her.

We know her likes and dislikes. We know what she looks like and the clothes she wears. And behind the looks the kind of person she is – her temperament and character. We don't know *everything* about Mrs Jones, but we know enough to form our opinions. She is there – just around the corner. We like her, but we don't worship her.

Let's move on a stage to one we do worship – Jesus. We worship Jesus as part of the Trinity of God because he gives us the best idea of what God is like. "He who has seen me has seen the Father," he said to the apostle Philip. (John 14v.9)

Jesus, unlike Mrs Jones. is not just around the corner. He has no physical presence. We don't see him with our eyes but he is not beyond our grasp.

With faith, people perceive him in their minds and hearts and feel the closeness of his loving presence in their lives. That's amazing if you think about it because although we know, from the New Testament, quite a bit of what he said and did during his three years in the limelight there are enormous gaps in the thirty three years of his life on earth which are lost to us. And the whole church is built on those brief years! How can this be?

To know Jesus is less easy than to know a Mrs Jones, but it is not impossible, given that so many people around the globe claim to *have* that relationship. But where do we begin with God and the person who asks us to describe God?

When I was teaching Religious Studies I would often use with older classes a text book with the intriguing title, "The Trouble with God!" The trouble with God, I suggest, is God himself. God is such a vast concept.

There's an ancient Hindu story of some blind men who were asked to describe an elephant.

They gathered round the towering animal and began to explore him with their hands.

The one who felt the head said that an elephant is a huge pot. The blind man who touched an ear announced that an elephant is large and rough, like a rug. The next man grasped the tusk and concluded that an elephant is like the cutting part of a plough.

Others felt the trunk and the powerful legs and feet and described the animal as a destructive pipe mounted on mighty, moving pillars.

The last man, who had clutched the elephant's tail, interrupted angrily. "You've *all* got it wrong! The elephant is like a broom for sweeping away its enemies.

The blind men fell out, and came to blows.

Their hearers soon took sides - each group asserting that only they had the truth. Of course no single person was wrong but each group had only part of the whole picture.

When we try to understand God we are like blind men feeling our way with a concept – a reality – which is too big for our limited understanding. Nonetheless we must continue to probe the immensity of this great Being whom we refer to as GOD.

It's a lifelong search, challenging and exciting, sometimes baffling and frustrating, raising questions and occasional doubts.

It is, however, through the persistence of the searching and the grappling with the doubts that deep, enduring faith is discovered. That is what the author of the book of Job was trying to get across.

"Can we by searching find God?" wonders Job.

"If I could pinpoint him I would go straight to his door!"

Elements of doubt will always persist, not to the actual existence of God (very few people in the world assert that there isn't a God), but with regard to the *nature* of God. It is interesting that the great Medieval Church scholars, such as Thomas Aquinas, were reluctant to claim any real knowledge of God. Only with caution were they prepared to speculate as to what God is like.

God is a mystery whose depths we attempt to plumb but only dimly begin to understand. Oh we try – and indeed we must. Our Muslim friends ascribe 99 names to God:

the Merciful, the Compassionate,
the Almighty, the Creator,
the Judge, the Majestic and so on.

Using a rosary with 33 beads a devout Muslim will work his way through the rosary three times, saying all these names as a reminder of the characteristics of Allah, the One God.

Christians and Jews also attempt to describe God - in the hymns and psalms for instance. It enhances our worship and feeds our faith. A hymn like "Immortal, Invisible" is a prime example. In adoration we tell God how we see him – immortal, invisible, almighty, victorious, unresting, unhasting, unchanging, eternal. Phrase is piled upon phrase as we acknowledge God to be the source of life, of goodness, of purity, of love and of splendour.

We may not use prayer beads as a vehicle of praise but it's not a bad idea to sometimes read through a hymn of praise in our personal devotions, especially when our faith is burning low and God seems far away. Praise helps us to focus on God and lifts our spirits.

One day a week is not enough to keep us going, as George Herbert reminds us:

"Seven whole days, not one in seven, I will praise thee; In my heart, though not yet in heaven, I can raise thee. Small it is, in this poor sort to enrol thee: Even eternity's too short to extol thee."

The poet is marvelling that weak human beings can connect with mighty God. It might seem unlikely that God can be worshipped in our feeble ways but even *we* can beam in to God. And Eternity itself would not be long enough to praise God adequately!

Let's pause there to sing that hymn now "King of glory, King of peace, I will love thee."

In that 17th century hymn The Search for God continues – and still does, and always will.

For George Herbert, God remained a mystery to be fathomed and praised. The descriptions of poets and hymn writers do help us because they personalise God and make concrete our thinking about him. They move us further on in our faith and understanding even though our concepts will still have limitations.

How can we explain, for instance, that God is personal and yet he is Spirit; that God is all loving and yet his children die from illnesses, disease, and natural disasters where no human factor can be blamed?

We call God "Father" but do not those who refer to God as "Mother" have a valid point?

Do you comprehend how God can be eternal? "Who made God?" I was often asked in the classroom. That is easy to dodge by pointing out that if someone made God you would have to ask, "Who made the someone who made God?" and "Who made the someone who made the someone who made God?" And so on...

It's like outer space really. What's at the end of space? If you travel far enough in your little space rocket will you reach some terminus? Will there be a wall with a sign reading "The end of space"? If so it won't be long before your curiosity makes you climb the wall to see what's at the other side. And what *could* there be at the other side except more space?

Space and time and God must go on for ever. God always has been and always will be. I don't understand how – but what alternative explanation could there be? And if you say "There isn't a God anyway," you can't apply that same sort of dismissive thinking to the mysteries of time and space.

"God is all powerful," some say. Could he commit suicide, self destruct? Could he contradict the natural laws of physics laid down from the foundations of the earth, which provide us with necessary order and stability, just to rescue us from harm if we accidentally fall in front of a moving train?

How does God, (who has all the world to look after), hear and respond to my often unimportant and self centred prayers? Little me, one in seven thousand million or so people?

Thinking about God involves us in all these intellectual gymnastics which is maybe why not many sermons are devoted solely to the subject of God.

In church we use the language of believers, but it's a foreign language to many folk – so there is a further problem for us to think about.

There is the story of an American tourist going to a cricket match in an attempt to understand our English culture. "Can you explain the game to me?" he asked the person sitting next to him.

"Oh it's perfectly simple," was the reply. "There are two teams. The team that bats first sends two players out to face the fielders who are already out.

When one of the batsmen is out he comes in and another batsman goes out and stays in until *he* is out. And so on. When the tenth player is out he comes in with his partner who is not out. The whole team is out now.

The fielding team then comes in because it's their turn to go out – and the batting team now goes out to field. The new batting team sends out their players in pairs until they are all out – except the eleventh batsman comes in being not out. The team that scores most runs wins.

That would be like a foreign language to an American and for many people it's a bit like that when they hear or read about God. We try to define the indefinable and it's not easy. But although we ourselves will never fully understand God it doesn't mean that he is unknowable or non existent. Indeed the testimony of hundreds of millions of believers of all Faiths (not just Christianity) is that God is real, loving and vital to our understanding of the world and of our lives.

When Trinity Sunday comes round some preachers quake a little at the thought because the idea of God in three Persons and yet remaining one God is difficult to explain to congregations.

The Trinity is hinted at in scripture but not spelled out as a definite doctrine. It was the Early Church in her wisdom who came to recognize three aspects of God:

God the Father who creates and loves;
God the Son who identifies with us
in the person of Jesus – the human
face of God;
and God the Spirit, whose joyful
presence in our lives
prompts us to faith, calls us to service
and leads us to know Jesus, to know God
and to experience on earth a foretaste of heaven.

The Trinity – one God in three Persons. Baffling, but *exciting*. Wow! Cricket could seem complicated and boring to the uninitiated but get to know a bit about it, persevere, and you might just come to appreciate some of its thrills.

It's like that with God and the Church. Sadly too many folk give up before they've begun. Perhaps we put them off! (There's a thought - and another sermon!)

Your task, and mine, is to stimulate thinking about God. We do that chiefly by just being good advertisements for the Christian faith. We're not on our own in this because the Holy Spirit (our Strengthener) will help us – without our realising it.

Opportunities arise each day for us to smile, to give a helping hand, to say a friendly word, to talk about our church or our faith. Now *that* is witnessing, or evangelism.

You don't need to be a preacher or be able to spout bible verses. That puts people off, as you know when the Jehovah's Witnesses stand on your doorstep.

Just be natural, be yourself. That's what God wants and if we love him then *be certain of this* – he wants us to share that love, to be his witnesses.

The question, "Who shall I send?" is not just addressed to prophets. "Here am I Lord," is a response we are all asked to make.

Isaiah's response came in the setting of worship. Whenever we worship we are in fact searching to know more about God. The good Pharisee, Nicodemus, was searching and so engaged Jesus in conversation, discovering that he too was required to make a commitment, to surrender himself to the Spirit of God.

Elsewhere the troubled believer portrayed in the character of Job cries in despair (and we've all been there): "God has no right to treat me like this," complains Job. It isn't fair!

I wish I knew where to find him.
I have searched everywhere...
but he is not there." (Job 23)

A lot of searching goes on in this thought provoking tale.

We are *all* involved in a search for the truth about God. We are *all* looking for God. But if God is so difficult a concept what hope is there of any success? Well thankfully one of the troubles with God, which I haven't mentioned yet, is that he will not let us go. Somehow or other the idea of God will not go away.

The trouble with God is that *he* troubles *us*. Even ardent atheists like Richard Dawkins want to talk about God! They put slogans on London buses which said, "Don't worry! There is no God."

Didn't they realize that just mentioning this supposedly non-existent God actually makes people think about him! (and possibly join in the search).

Jesus told many stories about searching – and finding. "The Kingdom of God is like a man looking for fine pearls who finds one and sells everything to buy it."

"The Kingdom of God is like a man who finds treasure in a field and sells everything he has to buy the field."

We do the searching: Seek and you will find" is the promise.

But how *can* we find God without any help? Surely it's an impossible task – like looking for the proverbial needle in a haystack. Well it would be were it not for the fact that it is not a one sided search – and here is the really good news:

Always, and even before we begin a conscious search for God, God is already there, searching for us.

So the Kingdom of God is also like a shepherd who goes out looking for his one foolish lost sheep and the Kingdom of God is like a heartbroken father daily standing at the end of the road waiting for his rebellious son to come to his senses and return home.

Like the relentless "hound of heaven" God pursues us through our rejections and rebellions, our griefs and our doubts, to embrace us with his love.

Sermons about God? Difficult! For as the Prologue to John's Gospel tells us: "No one has seen God. It is God the only Son, who is close to the Father's heart, who has made him known" (John 1v.18)

So God remains a mystery, but Jesus opens the door and invites us to enter and explore. If you really want to know God, or to know a bit more about him, then work on getting close to Jesus. "Whoever has seen me," said Jesus, "has seen the Father." (John 14v9)

So, let the search continue, in your life and in mine.

(Preached at Knutsford Methodist Church Feb 9th 2020. An earlier version at Adel Methodist on 19th January 2014)

TALES OF THE
UNEXPECTED

Just opposite the Headingley Cricket Ground in Leeds there is a flourishing Baptist church with a large roadside notice board in a very prominent position so that travellers in every passing bus and car and folk on foot on this busy road cannot fail to see its message.

It is put to very good use with thought provoking slogans which arrest the attention and are easy to remember. For example at Christmas time you may read "Jesus is the reason for the season" or "In those days wise men went looking for Jesus, wise people today still do." On another occasion there may be an invitation such as "Join us at our weekly celebration and enjoy good company, lively music, fine food – and wine"

Church notice boards can be a window into what we are all about and a challenge to passers by to think about their lives.They can be a means of presenting the Gospel with wit, humour and a hoped for response of "Well now! That's worth thinking about."

Great care has to be taken of course. There are lots of funny stories which may or may not be true –

such as the church which announced as its subject for Sunday "What is hell and what is it like?" but unwisely retained the regular invitation "Come and hear our choir"

Talking about sermon subjects and titles, reminds me of how, many years ago, I walked past a church whose notice board announced its coming Sunday sermon topic as "Mustard Seed and a Grain of Corn" and I asked myself whether that would have any meaning for the majority of the people passing by who would not have an agricultural background. But then I thought "Hang on Brian! Don't just criticise. What arresting sermon titles would *you* come up with?"

I began to look for topics that just about everybody in our land could identify with regardless of their gender, age, where they live, their upbringing, education, whatever. We all have our different interests so not everyone will be gripped by sports, or reading or politics but most of us will have opinions about what's on the telly. Television is the most common factor, so why not a series of sermons with titles of popular television programmes which can be linked with Christian and Biblical ideas?

I set myself the task of writing ten such sermons. Reaching for the Radio Times I began my search. I soon came up with "Neighbours" (you may have heard me preach that).

"Songs of Praise" explores not just that remarkably popular and long running series but also asks why Christians love singing together (especially Methodists!)

"Loose Women" is a possibility. There are plenty of those within our scriptures but before we men become too smug just consider "Men behaving Badly". There are far more accounts of male misdemeanours in the Bible. I don't know what people would make of it though if our notice boards advertised Loose Women this week followed by Badly Behaved Men next Sunday.

Running these ideas by a friend I received the suggestion that I should call my final ever sermon "Wanted Down Under". A twinkle in his eye reassured me that he wasn't referring to my eternal destination!

There are lots of other programmes which could be the starting point of a sermon. "Question Time," "Pointless," "The Weakest Link", "Open all Hours" are full of scope for not only praising or criticising the programme itself but also for exploring Christian perspectives on important issues which we all face in life.

"Cash in the Attic" could be linked with Jesus's teaching about treasures in heaven! See what suggestions *you* can come up with. You'll soon reach ten, especially if you go back to old favourites.

For me one *must-watch* weekly drama was "Tales of the Unexpected". Stories with a surprise twist in the tail.

I want to share with you three tales with unexpected endings. They're not from the TV series but you can catch up with the repeats which are still shown on some channels. The first of my stories is from an old school assembly book and is complete fiction; the second may have happened in some form or another in real life; the third is from my own career.

TALE NO 1 involves a train journey in the days of coal fired locomotives and carriages with the corridor down one side. Just as the train was about to pull out of the station a young man dashed along the platform and thankfully grabbed open the door and jumped in. He walked along the corridor until he found an empty compartment. Sitting down just inside he closed the sliding door and put his feet up on the seat opposite. "Good!" he thought. "A compartment to myself. I hate sharing with other people, who chatter and eat and disturb me. I'll just keep my legs stretched out and nobody will come in." He closed his eyes and smiled smugly.

At that very moment the door was slid open by a snooty looking young woman carrying a poodle. She glared down at his outstretched legs Slowly and reluctantly he put his feet on the floor allowing her to pass. Without a word of thanks she took her seat by the window, putting the dog on her lap.

The train moved off, the couple sitting in silent hostility. Suddenly she stood up and let down the window. An icy blast came rushing in and the young man drew his raincoat collar closer round his neck, saying:

"Excuse me but could we have the window closed. It's very draughty and I'm frozen?" "Oh! I'm quite warm" she replied and continued looking out of the window.

"Don't you think you're being rather selfish?" he asked. "After all, you didn't ask *me* whether I wanted the window open." She made no comment, ignoring him completely. Then he had an idea. Taking out his pipe and tobacco he lit up. Within seconds he was blowing great clouds of smoke into the air.

"Excuse me!" snorted the young woman. "It's the height of rudeness to smoke a filthy thing in an enclosed space in the presence of a stranger. Will you please put it out?" "No," said he and carried on puffing away with obvious enjoyment. She gave him a long angry stare. Then a slight smile crossed her lips.

She let the poodle slip from her lap to the floor. The little dog's first action was to trot across and sniff at the man's shoe. Then the dog licked it and, taking the shoelace in its teeth, tugged it loose.

"Will you please keep your dog under control?" "No!" was the answer, "and may I say you're the rudest person I've met for many a long day!"

"Ho!" he retorted "and you're the most self centred person I've ever had the misfortune to share a railway compartment with!"

Flushing with rage she got up, grabbed the pipe and threw it out of the window. Quick as a flash he picked up the poodle – and threw that out too.

They sat down, still annoyed but feeling a bit ashamed, and stared speechless at each other.

After a little while, when her anger had cooled, the young lady began to think that perhaps she had not behaved very well. At the same time the young man was beginning to feel sorry for his part in the argument.

Eventually they were able to apologise and even began to enjoy each other's company. When they reached their destination they stayed chatting on the platform. As they lingered guess what came running up to them. That's right – the poodle. And you'll never guess what he had in his mouth! ... Don't be silly. In his mouth was his tongue!

Well now. There's an unexpected ending or was it it a new beginning? (You add your own continuation).

TALE No 2 (Are you sitting comfortably?)

Somewhere in Huddersfield (I'm choosing Yorkshire places and people but you substitute your own – Manchester, Liverpool?)

Somewhere in Huddersfield an elderly lady went into a small café, bought a cup of tea and a two piece KitKat and sat down at the only available place, opposite a grim looking skinhead with a tattooed arm which read "Leeds United".

After arranging her handbag she reached out, broke the chocolate bar in half and ate the first piece. To her horror the skinhead's hand grasped the other half which was rapidly consumed. They glared at each other without saying a word.

Then the skinhead went to the counter to buy a cream bun. Putting it on the table he went back for a knife. With true Yorkshire grit the brave lady took a bite out of his bun while he was away.

Back he came, looked at his bitten bun, and then fiercely at the lady. Cutting off the bitten part he ate the rest, Silently smouldering he drank his tea and left Much relieved, our lady finished her drink and got up to go.

As she put her hand into her pocket for some change she found her own unopened KitKat and she realised it was the skinhead's chocolate she had eaten.

"Ee! That lad must think there's some funny fowk in 'Uddersfield!" she thought. Well now! There's another unexpected ending – or was it a new beginning? Perhaps the woman learned that we should not judge people by their appearance – by their dress, hairstyle, tattoes or the rings they wear in the nose, eyebrows or wherever.

Perhaps also she discovered that although there's some funny fowk in Huddersfield there's some even stranger ones in Leeds – but actually we're all fairly OK really. Oh, and that Leeds United are a better team than Huddersfield Town! (perhaps I should wait until the end of this season before saying that).

THE THIRD TALE is true and comes from my own experience as a teacher. Many years ago at Farnley Park High School in Leeds I ran a Community Service scheme. I used to visit a Mr and Mrs Alderson, for whom a couple of 16 year old lads did some gardening each week, as an alternative to Games. The Aldersons were well into their 80s and had been church goers all their lives. One day whilst reminiscing Mr Alderson told me of an incident way back in the 1920s which had stuck in his mind. He was waiting in the centre of

Leeds for a bus home some 3 miles away. It was a cold, miserable winter's night with wet slushy snow falling. A small, poorly dressed boy approached him with the question "Please mister can you spare an Halfpenny?" Mr Alderson only had tuppence, his bus fare, but the boy looked so pathetic that he gave him both coins. He then set off to walk the long uphill trudge home. After some 200 yards he passed the first gas lamp on Whitehall Road and noticed a glint of silver. Bending down he picked up half a crown. So his generosity had resulted in a profit of 2s and 4p in old money – a 15 fold increase. And he could now wait for the bus – a further bonus.

Another unexpected ending! And, who knows, perhaps a new beginning of some sort for the poor lad who was forced to beg.

Now Mr Alderson did not draw any divine magical or miraculous conclusions from that incident – and neither should we. But I reckon it is true in general that generosity brings its own rewards. Just as a mean, selfish person is likely to be unhappy, with few friends so the generous person who puts herself or himself out to help others has a better chance of finding happiness. There's a verse in Ecclesiastes (11v1), part of the Bible's Wisdom Literature, which says a similar thing: "Cast your bread upon the waters and it will return to you (increased)"

I remember from my youth Mrs Postill, a wise elderly Christian lady – a real Yorkshire character – who used to say "Chuck thi bread on't water and it'll come back to thee as Christmas cake!" That's an unexpected ending from the bible and there are hundreds of those. But at that point let's press the pause button to say a prayer and sing a hymn.

Loving Father, may we learn well from life's little incidents. Help us, like Jesus and his true followers to be generous with our our time and talents, our money and our possessions. Amen

"God has given us a book full of stories." So begins a children's hymn which you will not have sung since your Sunday School days. Stories make the Bible captivating and rich in meaning. They weren't just "made for the people of old" as the hymn states; the Bible is as relevant for today as it ever has been.

The gospels tell us that Jesus's favourite way of getting his message across was with an extensive use of stories – parables. A parable is a comparison such as the kingdom of heaven is like a grain of corn, or a mustard seed. A parable could also be a complete story as in that of the Prodigal Son.

Jesus, a master story teller, knew that parables capture then hold our attention. Challenging the hearers to work out a meaning, they remain in the memory. Parables are also timeless with a message for every age.

Stories Jesus told feature very prominently in the new Testament Gospels. That's not all the stories in a book which is full of stories and another huge chunk about Jesus are the accounts of the many miracles he performed. Then of course we get introduced to all the people Jesus met, many of them named. In addition we will have learned in some detail of the significant events in his life – birth stories, Bar Mitzvah, baptism, temptations, transfiguration, journey to the cross, and the tragic events of what we now call Holy Week.

I haven't covered the rest of the New Testament or any of the Old (the Hebrew scriptures) but enough has been said to justify the claim this is a "book full of stories."

And in all this wealth of stories you will find tales with unexpected outcomes, for God moves in mysterious ways his wonders to perform"

Lots of these surprise twists in the tail easily come to mind: Escape from Egypt when the Red Sea opens up; Goliath toppled by a shepherd boy's pebble; cowering Elijah comforted in the storm by God's still, small voice; 5000 hungry people somehow being fed after a young lad offered his picnic; a runaway son coming to his senses and going back home to say sorry.

Who would have thought that such happy endings could come to rescue such impossible situations? All these tales of the unexpected do not make sense unless they are making a point and of course they are.

The writers want us to know that God steps into the ordinary and the sometimes difficult or disastrous circumstances of our lives with his love and understanding. He comes to be alongside us, to encourage us, to lift us up, to rescue us, to weep with us, to shield us from our frailties and limitations by showing us that with Him no situation, no matter how dire, is beyond hope.

Which is why, of all these stories, the resurrection of Jesus is the most unexpected, the most surprising and the most glorious.

We sing now, joyfully, of that transforming Easter Day in our next hymn:

"See, what a morning, gloriously bright, with the dawning of hope in Jerusalem"

(Preached at Mobberley Methodist Church 1st September 2019)

THE ASCENSION

When Luke finished his gospel with a brief mention of the Ascension of Jesus his readers must have been asking, "What happened next? Is there a sequel?" Sure enough, with the skills of a modern writer or TV dramatist, Luke goes on to produce the second part of his story, the so called Acts of the Apostles. He begins this Part II with a more detailed account of the Ascension. It's a reminder to his sponsor, Theophilus (to whom both books are addressed), of the story so far, i.e. the birth, ministry, arrest, execution, resurrection and ascension of Jesus. Theophilus, a Roman nobleman, had asked for all the details. The opening of Acts is in effect saying, "Let's take up the story where we left off." The Ascension of Jesus is the link pin between Luke's two books.

It is interesting that Luke is the only New Testament author to describe the Ascension – an event which was to become an important festival in the Church's calendar and a key statement of belief in the historic Creeds. It raises questions for us today as to whether Luke was recording an accurate-in-every-detail historical event, or was he telling us deep truths about Jesus through the skilful use of his artistic and lively imagination? The modern reader has to decide whether this important story is purely metaphorical or a literal account, or a mixture of both. The more important question though is: "What does the Ascension reveal about Jesus, regardless of what we think of the historicity of Luke's account?"

The last time I preached about the Ascension I was tackled afterwards by a Baptist lay preacher who told me he agreed with much of what I had said, but added that he personally accepted the literal truth of that story. That's fair enough and it was refreshing that we could agree to disagree and remain on friendly terms. I have no doubt that what I say today may raise similar concerns in some minds but I see part of a preacher's role is to not just give answers but sometimes to challenge long held beliefs and assumptions, which is after all what Jesus did. Do not be afraid therefore of engaging in such dialogues with preachers at the end of a service, be they ordained ministers or lay.

As a writer Luke was a master craftsman, which is why the Prodigal Son and the Good Samaritan parables are world famous short stories. It has been suggested that at the back of Luke's mind was the story of the ascension of the prophet Elijah (which was read to us earlier). Was Luke in effect saying that Jesus was greater even than the greatest Jewish Prophet, Elijah?

Elijah was taken to heaven in a chariot of fire. According to Luke, Jesus needed no such help but ascended on his own. Elijah's disciple, Elisha, received a double portion of his master's spirit, but the disciples of Jesus received the infinite power of God's Holy Spirit which we will joyfully celebrate in a few days' time on Pentecost Sunday. Luke was leading his readers to that significant event when the Church was born as the Holy Spirit came not just to one lone disciple as with Elijah and Elisha but to the whole assembled group of the disciples of Jesus and from then onwards cascading out to those choosing to be followers of Jesus in every century and all over the world.

Crucifixion, Resurrection, Ascension and the baptism of the Holy Spirit – that for Luke was an essential sequence. There *just had to be* a farewell appearance of Jesus. He couldn't have jumped straight from Easter to Pentecost. So there had to be the Ascension. The intervening period of 40 days, during which Jesus appeared to his disciples ("by many convincing proofs" Luke tells us in his follow up) is not only peculiar to this evangelist but is another reference to events in Jewish scriptures, offering further evidence that Jesus was God's Messiah. We would love to know a bit more about that time of resurrection appearances and the teachings of the risen Christ.

The Ascension then. Is it total fact or an ingenious literary device used by Luke to bring out important truths about Jesus, the Christ? You must make up your own minds and if your approach to the Bible is a literal and inerrant one then I respect your views. For me, however, a literal reading of the Ascension presents difficulties and perhaps you will allow me to briefly mention some of these and at the same time to say why I think the story and the festival are so important – and also why it is a matter of regret that the nonconformist churches in particular have neglected to observe the celebrations.

I remember seeing a painting of the Ascension which showed Jesus's disciples gazing up to the skies at a cloud. Sticking out from the bottom of the cloud were the two feet of Jesus on his heavenward journey. Going on the internet I found 147 Ascension paintings by famous artists. Altogether there were three paintings with dangling feet, one of which had matching footprints on the ground below! Quite comical really but some of the artists and certainly the readers of Luke viewed the cosmos through pre-scientific lenses. Jewish scriptures portray a flat earth covered by a sky dome. God dwelt above the dome in heaven and Jesus ascended in order to go through the keyhole in the sky, to be enthroned at God's right hand. People in those far off days had no idea of the vastness of space or the possibility of space travel. If Jesus ascended physically into the sky even at the speed of light (186,000 miles per second) he would not yet have reached the edges of our own galaxy – and there are trillions of galaxies beyond ours! It is obvious then that a literal ascension and a physical location of heaven are no longer tenable to our 21st century knowledge of cosmology.

How then can we interpret the Ascension for modern minds? And can we observe the festival if we have so many unanswered questions as to its historical authenticity? Well, do we not celebrate Christmas with great enthusiasm, even though we recognise that many details in the narratives are metaphorical and symbolic? Does it really matter if angels serenading shepherds and wise men following a moving star are inventions? It's what they are telling us about Jesus that's important, and often parable and metaphor can express deep truths which a literal approach would obscure. Such, I believe is the case with the Ascension.

I share with you some of those truths which bible scholars suggest Luke was trying to convey to his readers. For Luke there had to be a moment when the sudden, spasmodic appearances, such as on the Emmaus Road, behind locked doors in the upper room, or on the shores of Galilee, would cease. There had to be a final farewell to the physical form of Jesus, and this was it – his Ascension, his day of glory. This was the moment when the Jesus of earth became the Christ of Heaven.

If you visit Coventry Cathedral you cannot miss the Graham Sutherland tapestry of Jesus seated in glory because it is above the high altar for all to see as the cathedral is entered. It is claimed to be the largest tapestry in the world. Your eyes are immediately drawn to it.The tapestry may not appeal to you but, whatever impression it makes, the idea is surely right – that the risen, ascended and glorified Lord Jesus should be high and lifted up in the Church's life and worship.

"Keep your eyes fixed on Jesus," says the letter to the Hebrews. (12v1-2) The danger is that sometimes in our plethora of church meetings and the reorganisation of circuits, (necessary though that might be), we can get so bogged down with details and extra work that we take our eyes off Jesus and fail to magnify him and give him the highest priority.

The Ascension reminds us that we serve a glorified Lord who must be at the centre of not just our worship, but of all that we do together as a church community. I confess that in my moments of tiredness and disappointment I sometimes forget this and my faith wobbles.

In Luke's scenario the Ascension gave glory to Jesus. Perhaps a better word for ascension would be exaltation. Luke does say that Jesus was "lifted up" but the phrase "was carried into heaven" is not in his original version. Someone else added those words much later. So Luke could have been saying that Jesus was lifted up in the sense of becoming worthy of worship – just as in *our* worship we seek to exalt Jesus, to lift him up for all to acknowledge and praise. The Sovereignty of Christ is a way to express this in words and the Coventry Cathedral tapestry is a visual presentation of the same idea.

The cloud which enveloped Jesus is also significant. It would remind Luke's readers of the cloud on Mount Sinai in Moses' day, wherein dwelt God's glory. When the cloud dispersed at the Ascension Jesus had gone. The disciples knew that they would not see him again but for them, and for us, his absence would actually lead to the completion of his presence in our lives, and he will always be filled with glory.

An old hymn puts it well:"I see thee not, I hear thee not, yet thou art oft with me; And though I have not seen and still must rest in faith alone; I love thee dearest Lord, and will – Unseen, but not unknown."

The Ascension was a time of glory for Jesus and also a moment of gladness and graduation for the disciples. They didn't go home biting their nails, anxiously asking, "What's going to happen next?" Luke tells us that "they returned to Jerusalem with great joy, and spent all their time in the Temple praising God." No fearful uncertainty there! Gladness was a consequence of the Ascension. Praising God filled them with gladness and joy, (as it should us) because for the disciples the Ascension was also their day of graduation. I borrow that description from a meditation by Dick Williams:

"How wonderful Lord that you should leave the disciples to stand on their own feet; that you should not keep them tied to your apron strings.

This was their graduation day."

Occasionally when pupils were misbehaving in my classroom I would put on view a sign which read in large letters: GROW UP. Parents of teenagers may experience occasions when they wish their youngsters would grow up. Don't worry! The time will come when they emerge into adulthood – and sighs of relief are breathed on both sides. In some ways, of course, we all retain certain immaturities even in much later years but in general somewhere we cross the threshold into grownupness. We graduate into maturity, though in some of our thinking and attitudes we may still need to grow up. Especially this is true on a spiritual level, otherwise why would we need to have prayers of confession every Sunday?

With the Ascension of Jesus came the graduation of the disciples. In one sense the earthbound Jesus became redundant. His earthly ministry was over. They no longer needed to see him with their eyes. Jesus was handing over the reins and from then on they had to stand on their own feet. They had graduated. They were grown up.

Glory for Jesus with Gladness and Graduation for the disciples. The disciples still needed help though and that's where a fourth G word comes into the Ascension recipe. The Ascension for the disciples was a time of Guarantees. Those guarantees came from Jesus himself in the form of three promises within four verses in the first chapter of Acts. Jesus told them to stay in Jerusalem for "You will be baptized by the Holy Spirit not many days from now." (There's the first guarantee). "You will receive power when the Holy Spirit has come upon you." (the second). And the third guarantee from Jesus is "You will be my witnesses in Jerusalem, in all Judea and Samaria, and to the ends of the earth."

A story about a great conductor will complete our thoughts this morning. When Toscanini retired his orchestra broke up. Sometime later, a group of his musicians met together and decided to re-form. They booked a concert hall. They persuaded the others. They rehearsed. They publicised the event. On the night of the performance the orchestra was assembled on the stage. To the astonishment of the audience there was no conductor. The leader gave a nod and the orchestra began to play. As they played they relaxed and the guiding genius of Toscanini once more seemed at hand.

The concert was a huge success. The orchestra was a living unity, bound together by the spirit of the master.

So is the Church bound together by the spirit of *her* master. Jesus is present within his church. He guaranteed that! Like those first disciples in Luke's Ascension story may we too know the glory of our risen Lord. May we share their gladness and their sense of graduation as we take to heart those guarantees which our master Jesus still gives.

Also like them let us get on with sharing all this good news. Pentecost comes next Sunday to complete Luke's cycle of those world shattering events at the climax of Jesus's life – Pentecost or Whit Sunday when we remember the invigorating power of the Holy Spirit and the launching of the Church. Wow!! Now that is a festival to celebrate. Be here!

(Preached at Headingley Methodist Church, Leeds on 20th May 2013)

A SERIES OF
UNFORTUNATE INCIDENTS

Do you ever think of yourself as a "chip off the old block"? You will know what I mean because, like it or not, each one of us inherits not just physical features from our parents but also mannerisms, talents and skills, personality traits, both desirable and off putting. Voice and walking patterns too will be recognised by family friends.

When your wife or husband says to you, "You're just like your mum or dad!" you will know from their tone of voice whether it's a criticism or a compliment. For your sake I hope it's the latter, otherwise you are in trouble!

When I was a young lad starting to take an interest in girls a wise man at my church who ran our Youth Fellowship gave this bit of good advice. "Lads," he said, "When you've been taken to meet her family and you are "getting your feet under the table," (as they used to say), take note of her mother and tell yourself that in twenty or so years' time your girlfriend will be just like her." Thankfully something must have registered because we eventually broke up (*she* ditched *me* actually!) My next girlfriend's mother was lovely. Patricia and I were married in due course and Patricia, just like her mum, was lovely too, and our two daughters have followed suit.

I thank God for my own mum and dad. Bringing up three children during those six wartime years could not have been easy. Dad worked on a farm and therefore was exempt from army service but he was off work for two years with stomach ulcers so not much money was coming in. Most families struggled with poverty as well as all the restrictions imposed by that terrible war.

It's telling how coronavirus has stirred up memories from that distant childhood – and regrets that I wasn't old enough to fully appreciate all the sacrifices and love of anxious parents for their precious children.

My mother outlived dad by some 13 years and did not take kindly to old age with its loneliness, and the aches and pains of arthritis. "It's no fun growing old" she often said but when she limped into the kitchen of her high rise flat in Leeds we could hear her singing the melody of "Thine be the glory". So there must have been some joy for her in the melancholy of old age.

I know not whether I have inherited the same chips from *my* old blocks but I reflect on my mother's words and conclude that actually there are lots of bits of fun in growing old, to counterbalance the inevitable drawbacks. Hopefully there is a modicum of wisdom acquired from your own experiences (and mistakes). "Nous" (rhymes with mouse) we call it in Yorkshire – common sense which can and should be shared with younger folk.

There is also a whole treasure chest of happy memories filled with family and friends, to be dipped into when we are feeling down. And for those of us who are fortunate enough there will be grandchildren. If membership of the grandparents club has not been *your* privilege perhaps you will have nieces, nephews, children of friends to whom you have been an "auntie or uncle."

Most of us enter old age knowing children who are special to us – whom we have cradled in our arms as babies, whose journeys through childhood, adolescence and careers we have followed with interest and prayers and who now may be producing their own little chips off the old block for us to dote over. So life passes by but the saga carries on.

It has been said that "nobody can do for children what grandparents (and such) do. They sort of sprinkle stardust over their young lives." Even though the stardust sometimes seems to be a bit expensive we grin and tell ourselves "They are worth it!" There are many bonuses for us along the way.

I remember going to school nativity plays, eating out at a Pizza Hut, venturing on at least some of the rides at a Theme Park, shouting out "Oh Yes it is!" at a pantomime, falling asleep at the cinema after all the popcorn had gone and I was pretending to watch "Stuart Little Two", standing on the touchline on a cold day watching a grandson playing rugby for his school. You will have your own treasured memories.

One week in particular sticks in my mind. Our Knutsford grand daughter was with us in Leeds for a half term week. She was only eight or nine at the time (she is now in her mid-20s).She was easy to entertain but we had to think of some special treats. One was a visit to the cinema and the other to a matinee at the West Yorkshire Playhouse.

The film was "A Series of Unfortunate Events" based on three of a number of books for children written by Lemony Snicket. At the beginning of the first of the eleven books the author gives this warning: "The book you are holding in your hands is extremely unpleasant. It tells an unhappy tale about three very unlucky children. Even though they are charming and clever, the Beaudelaire siblings lead lives filled with misery and woe. From the very first page when the children are at the beach where they receive terrible news, disaster lurks at their heels and continues through the entire story. One might say they are magnets for misfortune. It is my sad duty to write down these unpleasant tales but there is nothing stopping you from putting this book down at once and reading something happy, if you prefer."

Well now that seems rather off-putting doesn't it? Not exactly designed to make you want to read on! But surprisingly children do read on and enjoy the series. Perhaps it's the exciting pace which makes the books so popular, and the hint that eventually the villains will get their come-uppance and the Baudelaire children, who are learning through each experience, will ultimately be OK. The author also uses some big words which are explained without interrupting the flow.

It all starts with a fire at the rather large and smart Baudelaire mansion. The three children, Violet, Klaus and Sunny aged 14, 12 and one are at the nearby beach, with instructions to return home for lunch. Their play is interrupted by the arrival of Mr Poe, family friend and bank official. "I'm afraid I have some very bad news for you children," he tells them. "Your parents have perished in a terrible fire which has destroyed the whole house."

Mr Poe is the executor of their parents' estate, although Violet feels at that moment that "executioner" would be a more fitting word. (Three of those big words there) So the children, who have lost their parents and all their belongings – toys, clothes, books, in a single morning, become orphans, looked after at first by Mr and Mrs Poe who have two loud and obnoxious boys. The food is unappetising (cold porridge for instance), their rooms are cramped, the clothes bought for them are itching and in grotesque colours, and the Baudelaire children are very unhappy.

They are then sent to live with a previously unknown distant relative (Count Olaf) and their situation goes from bad to worse because their new guardian turns out to be not a real Count but an impoverished eccentric actor who begins to plot "accidents" to his charges so that he can inherit the considerable family fortune. The film makes the most of dramatic scenes: the children are left in a locked car on a railway crossing, in the path of an express train; they are in a cliff top house which collapses into the sea; they are in a rowing boat which is attacked by giant man eating fish. But I'll not reveal any more spoilers because you may catch one of the TV repeats.

Now, for those of you who are wondering where the Christian sermon is in all this, listen up. It has occurred to me that the title "A Series of Unfortunate Incidents" could be given to another epic saga which we hear bits of every Sunday in church and, if we are wise and brave enough, will dip into for our personal reading at other times too – THE BIBLE.

The Bible seems to consist of one episode after another where things unfortunately go wrong – right from the third chapter of the first book with the meaningful folktale of Adam and Evebeing kicked out of their paradise Garden because they couldn't follow simple basic rules. The trend is set: a disastrous flood with only Noah's crew surviving; a Tower of Babel collapsing and causing chaos because human beings had gotten above themselves. Many of these early stories were parables – powerful myths teaching important truths for all times (even or maybe especially for today) about life and about God.

The real history of the Jewish nation then begins with Abraham, followed by Isaac, Jacob and an arrogant Joseph being sold into Egypt by his jealous brothers. All of which ends up in slavery for the entire nation of God's "chosen race" – the children of Israel. Freedom after years of hardship only leads to 40 miserable years in the wilderness. Even after settling in their Promised Land more suffering was to come from surrounding enemies and from a succession of their own inadequate rulers.

There are moments of triumph in the Old Testament but, by and large, hardship and disaster seem to predominate: evil kings undo the work of good kings, prophets are ignored, or punished, Temples are built and destroyed. Jews are carted off into foreign exile and Israel is reduced to a downtrodden country under the heel of the mighty Roman Empire. That's where the New Testament begins.

I need to stress at this point that the light and the hope bubbling under the surface of all the sorry history in the Hebrew Scriptures are of course NOT blotted out in the Christian Holy Book. On the contrary!

It is, however, possible to sum up the New Testament in a negative way. You might think that I just applied the same approach to the Old Testament but I would contest that. Opponents of the Christian faith may conclude that Jesus did not fulfil the popular expectations of a Jewish Messiah, or a Saviour of the World, pointing out that Palm Sunday's cheers of delight soon gave way to Good Friday's jeers of derision and that to our Jewish friends it is inconceivable that God's special rescuer could end up dead on an executioner's cross. For one thing it contradicts their scripture "cursed is he who hangs on a tree." (Deut 21v.23) Anyway dead means dead.

These are the sort of challenges we Christians have to grapple with. Baffling – but exciting isn't it? The Bible then – a series of unfortunate incidents of spectacular proportions but also of staggering assurances of divine love and support.

Why is the Bible the world's best-selling and most read book? Why do we hear it every Sunday in church? Well, perhaps like Lemony Snicket's book, it has an exciting pace, a rich style of writing (though there are boring bits) and always the hint that evil will not have the last word.

The second treat we gave our grand daughter was to see the theatre production "The Lion, the Witch and the Wardrobe," a play based on one of the seven Chronicles of Narnia by C.S. Lewis published as long ago as the 1950s and immensely popular with children and adults. There can't be many of you who have not read the books or come across the story in films or on the TV. I am a fan of CS Lewis and could go into great detail but will resist the temptation otherwise this sermon will double in length.

I *will* just remind you though that it's about four children who go through the back of an old wardrobe to find themselves in the magical world of Narnia in a land of talking animals which is under the cruel reign of the evil White Witch with her powerful armies of giants, hags, ogres and fierce wolves. She has introduced a permanent winter with ice and snow everywhere. It is always winter but never Christmas. After many struggles, rescue eventually comes through the arrival of a long prophesied Saviour – the magnificent Lion, Aslan, but not without great cost. To save one of the children Aslan offers *himself* as a sacrifice and is bound up on a large stone table. The Queen plunges her knife into his heart. The children and the talking animals are devastated and heartbroken.

When the two girls return at dawn a couple of days later, to untie Aslan's ropes and bathe his wounds, they find that the stone table has been broken and the body removed. They hear a gentle growl and a booming voice. Lo! There is Aslan restored to life! It reminds us of course of the crucified and risen Jesus. The author does not specifically write that but there is no doubt that the great Bible themes lie behind the Narnia Chronicles: good triumphing over evil, despair being overcome by hope, death defeated.

Why not while away your summer days or winter evenings by reading again the Chronicles of Narnia – or perhaps for the first time!

In concluding I want to link up with my opening comments about chips and old blocks. One of the frustrations of our Covid-19 isolating and distancing measures has been our inability to greet others with a handshake. To get round this some adopted the Indian custom of Namaste where you place your hands together in prayer-like fashion and bow your head. It is a way of saying "Hello or peace or shalom". Hindu religious ideas include the belief that within each human being and animal there is a bit of God. The word namaste means "bow" so when you say "Namaste" it is really the Divine in you which is bowing to the Divine in your neighbour. I find that to be a lovely notion and I wonder whether that is behind some of the Bible's teaching. For instance when Genesis suggests that we are made in the image of God, or when Jesus, towards the end of John's Gospel, breathes the Holy Spirit into the frightened disciples' lives and when Paul reminds his sceptical audience in Athens of the words of the Greek poets that "in Him we all live and move and have our being". If God is our maker, as we claim, is it not conceivable that we should bear the marks of our master artist – just as art critics can spot the paintings of say Rembrandt, Van Gogh, El Greco by looking carefully at the work before them? In this way we carry within us a spark of the Divine. We are chips off the Old Block.

I read somewhere of Mother Teresa of Calcutta being asked how she could possibly wash and dress the wounds of diseased, filthy and fetid lepers. She replied that she was seeing and treating the Christ within each one of them.

When I say Namaste to you I am not trying to import foreign religious beliefs into Christianity, to create what they call a syncretistic religion with watered down beliefs. I am simply acknowledging that the essence of God within me recognises that the Divine also resides in you. The parable at the end of Matthew 25 – with the words "Whatever you did to the least of my family you did to me" seems to reinforce this idea.

So then, "Namaste!" God bless you and may we all be Christ centred and Spirit led for we are chips off the old block and that's how God would have us be. AMEN

(Preached at Whingate Methodist Church, Leeds on the27 Feb 2005 and at Mobberley Methodist Sept 1st 2019)

WOBBLY MOMENTS
AND EMPTY VESSELS

It is strange how unimportant incidents often lodge in the memory and can be recalled quite clearly after many, many years. I can understand why I remember momentous occasions in my early life such as the street bonfire on VJ Day, sitting my 11 plus exam on a very snowy day, my first day at High School, our family cat having to be put down the day before King George VI died (what a sad week that was!). I remember being the sixth pair of legs in a prehistoric monster in our local carnival, the Coronation of our Queen, starting work at Bramley station, my square bashing as a far from enthusiastic National Serviceman…. (I'll stop there before the violins come out!)

All of these were significant events which made a big impact on me so it is quite understandable that I should not forget them. But why should a few seemingly trivial happenings sometimes return to mind with clarity as though they had taken place only yesterday? Is it the same with you, or am I the only one that's odd round here. (Don't answer that!) Invariably something triggers their recall – a conversation, a sentence in a book, a television picture perhaps. It was a parable of

Jesus which was responsible for me remembering two such unconnected incidents from the vague, shadowy mists of a distant and fast receding childhood. (I'm going back more than 70 years!)

I was coming home from school in the centre of Leeds and the bus, (or was it a tram?) was crowded. I found a seat upstairs right at the back. I was on the left side – as was a man sitting next to the aisle a few seats in front of the exit. He had obviously been playing snooker because his cue was in a metal tube which he held upright in his right hand. As the journey continued people started to get off. They came down the aisle to the steps exit at the rear. You can guess what happened. Person after person, eyes on the steps, grasped the tube, mistaking it for a passenger floor to ceiling rail. The startled looks on their faces when the presumed hand rail wobbled was highly comical. They were wobbly moments.

The second incident took place near Bramley Town End. It was a summer evening and I was walking home after choir practice at the church of the Venerable Bede, where I was a boy chorister. I spotted a ball of wool on the ground gently rolling down the hill towards me – an unwinding ball of wool. I followed the strand some 20 or so yards to a woman walking away totally unaware that the ball of wool had dropped out of her shopping basket (Do you remember those?)

It was this latter triviality that came to mind years later when I read this parable of Jesus:

"The Kingdom is like a certain woman who was carrying a jar full of meal. (It was probably barley for baking bread and maybe the earthenware jar was on her shoulder). *While she was walking along, still some distance from home a handle of the jar broke and the meal began to trickle out. When she reached her house, she set the jar down and found it empty."*

That parable may be new to you because it's not in the New Testament. It comes from the late second century Gospel of Thomas – a collection of sayings of Jesus many of which are paralleled in the Gospels of Matthew, Mark and Luke. Scholars were aware of a few Greek fragments from Thomas going back to about 200 AD but there was great excitement in 1945 when a Coptic scroll of the complete Gospel of Thomas was discovered in desert excavations in Egypt.

It's a vivid little parable isn't it? You can see this woman walking along quite unaware of what has happened. We are not given any details but the earthenware jar may have been tied on her back somehow, with a rope fastened to each handle and one handle broke allowing the jar to tilt and the contents to spill out. It's odd that she didn't notice it. Her mind must have been on other things. We can imagine her shock and dismay when she reached home ready to get on with the baking, only to find that her chief ingredient was missing! The jar was empty! Money would be scarce. Maybe the family had to go hungry that day.

How often, ladies, do you get half way through mixing a recipe and you say, "Ah! I see I need some currants. I'll just get some from the cupboard." You open the door and the jar is empty! That's where one of those precious items called husbands (or children) is handy. In your sweetest voice you say, "Dearie, will you slip out to the shop for me please?" Husband, who is reading his newspaper, (or child who is playing games on a laptop) ask, "Will this afternoon do? "No! Now! I'm out of essentials and it's urgent. The currant jar is empty!"

I give this sermon a title: "Empty Vessels," and I preach it as a warning to all of us, myself included (nay especially to myself) – a warning of the dangers of becoming empty vessels, as far as our faith and our enthusiasm and our love for our Lord are concerned.

With that unstable snooker cue tube in mind I extend the title to "Empty Vessels and Wobbly Moments." Having wobbly moments in our faith (and they come to all of us at times) could be a consequence of our spiritual resources running low, even on empty.

Switching analogies, I remember some years ago my wife Patricia and I driving up from Pembrokeshire in South Wales to the Lleyn Peninsula in mid Wales. After a holiday with friends who lived in the little village of Marloes we were adding a few days at a cottage in Neffyn in mid Wales. It was Sunday and I made the mistake of not filling up with petrol before we set off. By late afternoon we were heading into the Welsh mountains.

"Better get some fuel," I thought, so we diverted into a town to find that not only were the pubs dry on "the Sabbath" but the petrol stations (and everything else it seemed) were closed. We carried on, rueing the petrol we had wasted with that diversion. It was getting dark. Headlights were needed as we negotiated those unlit winding roads, flanked with forests, behind which lurked towering hills which we could no longer see, but whose looming and ominous presence we could feel. It was rather scary and when the needle touched the red, empty zone I was accutely anxious that the engine would shortly splutter and die and we would have to spend the night in those black mountains. It was like a scene from a horror movie. I was metaphorically kicking myself, thinking "failure" and trying to apologise to my long suffering and lovely wife. A few miles farther on, trying not to press too hard on the accelerator, we reached the top of a hill and at the bottom of the long straight road before us we espied the lights of an open petrol station. "Whew!" Was I relieved to reach the pump and get filled up. My empty tank had certainly given me more than a few anxious wobbles.

When you first heard Thomas's empty vessel parable you probably thought of the parable of the Lost Coin in Luke, read for us earlier. Both involve a woman, anxiety and something very important that gets lost. Both are illustrations of the Kingdom but the precious coin is lost and then found and there is great rejoicing, whereas the precious grain is lost for ever.

In Luke's story we can see where the Kingdom comes in. When sinners repent and the lost are found there is joy in heaven and in the Church on earth. We are glad when new disciples are made. But in Thomas there is no joy. Surely, you may think, the Kingdom of God is not an emptying but a filling, not about losing but about finding! True, but some of the parables of Jesus work in reverse or by contrast and some parables are a *warning* to his followers rather than an invitation to *become* a follower. This parable, therefore, may have a message to us, 21st century disciples or followers of Jesus, in an age which largely ignores him.

It is so easy for us to become an emptying or empty vessel, to become ineffective in our faith and witness. There are periods for all of us when our faith burns low, when doubts loom large, when circumstances overwhelm us and God seems far away. What can we do when we find ourselves in this "wilderness state"? Well, I have no glib and easy answers because we are all so different. Our circumstances, our temperaments, our state of health are unique to each one of us. We cannot fully stand in other people's shoes no matter how much we try to empathise.

I can make a few general and random suggestions and I'll try to do that. I find that hymns which deal with conflict, suffering and doubt (especially, but not only, the more modern ones) can be really relevant to some of our situations in recent times. Two hymns "When our confidence is shaken…" and "When, O God, our faith is tested.." ring bells with me and may help you. Catch some of the insights given:

When your confidence is shaken – wobbly in fact; when your spirit is paralysed with inertia and you cannot pick yourself up, remind yourself that (I'm quoting here) "God is active in the tensions of your faith". He may seem in the shadows but he is still there. When your faith is "tested and your hope is undermined and your love of living shrivels" and you ask God "Why?" and you are in an empty vessel state, does the prayer asking God "Are you with us in our grief?" lead you like the hymn writer to simply pray "Help us in our unbelief"?

When the challenges of ethical issues and the political posturing and aggressive language of Donald Trump and his supporters fill you with dread, threatening to undermine what you thought was a sure faith already having to cope with coronavirus, climate change and forecasts of severe recession then, indeed NOW, it is vitally important that we hold on to the insights we have received over years of worship. We must not give up the practice of prayer or the conviction handed down to us over the centuries that God is Love. He is the eternal answer to the world's eternal "Why?" For the sake of the world and future generations of the worldwide Church we have to hang in there even when at times our prayers may feel like "Oh God, if there is a God."

I believe that God honours our questioning and our honest doubts. As the hymn says, through such trials our faith matures and we learn to accept fresh insights. But it is not an easy road.

Finally, a three minute lesson in the 3 R's – not reading, writing and 'rithmetic, but remembering, recognising and rejoicing.

The command to remember appears a number of times in the Bible. The two most significant are these:"Remember that you were slaves in the land of Egypt and the Lord your God redeemed you." That is from Deuteronomy and is precious to Jews everywhere as at their annual Pesach or Passover meal they re-enact and re-live the Exodus story.

The other key verse is equally precious to Christians. They are the words of Jesus heard at every Communion Service:"Do this in remembrance of me." One of the most widely obeyed commands in human history.

The second R word is *Recognising*. In our empty and wobbly moments we must recognise that it is faith that matters, not feelings. God is the rock on which your faith has been built over the years. God is solid rock, not shifting sands. It might not feel like that when your confidence is shaken but faith does not depend on feelings. Feelings are affected by circumstances often beyond our control. The surface of a sea is sometimes tempestuous with huge waves but deep down, below all the turbulence, there is a calm stillness. Relying solely on our feelings can be devastating for us if we fail to recognise that deep within our own quaking and fearful souls lies the peace of God's calm. God's word to us is "Be still and know that I am God."(Psalm 46)

The third R is *Rejoicing*. Read again Paul's short letter to the Philippians which was written from a state of house imprisonment. "Rejoice in the Lord always and again I say rejoice... I have learned, in whatever state I am, to be content." And sing again Nahum

Tate's hymn: Through all the changing scenes of life, in trouble and in joy, the praises of my God shall still my heart and tongue employ."

Are you running on empty, in need of a refill? Are you experiencing wobbly moments? Well, you are in church this morning surrounded by Christian friends – and that is a very good place to be (in spite of the preacher!) Furthermore, our worship every Sunday celebrates the victories of Jesus – and that is a very good thing to do.

So then, off we go into another week *remembering, recognizing, and rejoicing!*

(Preached at churches in the Leeds West Circuit in 2013)

WHY DO CHRISTIANS SING?

During the coronavirus lockdown isolated Christians turned to the television and digital devices for the strength and solace of communal worship which Sunday services provide and which we really missed. Churches made valiant and praise worthy efforts to produce online sermons and acts of worship, some of which were ingenious and gave opportunities for the development of skills and talents of individuals and groups. Well done folk. You deserve our round of applause! Ways of worship in the future will surely see some changes because of these innovative ideas. Useful and inspiring as they were though such alternative worship was only a stopgap. We longed for the time when normal services would be resumed where we could meet with our friends again, shake hands, share bread and wine and chat over coffee afterwards. I guess too that most of us missed singing together hymns and worship songs accompanied by the organ or the music of the worship group. BBC's morning services and *Songs of Praise* were a good substitute but watching by yourself could not remove the sense of aloneness.

Look up *Songs of Praise* on the internet and you will be surprised by the information given. The first appearance was way back in 1961 and it's one of the longest running television series of its kind anywhere in the world with around two and a half thousand episodes. It is regularly shown in the Netherlands, New Zealand and Australia. It has visited in the region of 2000 churches, cathedrals and chapels as well as numerous outdoor locations. Audiences are invited.

I remember singing at the Harrogate Show Ground one summer for a pre-recorded Harvest Festival. We had to sing *Shine Jesus Shine* about ten times because the bandstand was in the middle of the arena, with the audience around the edges, and we couldn't get the timing synchronized.

We also went to a live broadcast, standing in the Millennium Square Leeds behind the iconic Town Hall which was filled with Brass Bands, leaving no room for an indoor audience. Inside we would have needed ear mufflers! Thankfully the weather was fine on both of those occasions.

The largest event was at the Millennium Stadium in Cardiff on the first Sunday in the year 2000 when over 60,000 people came to sing hymns, led by a choir of 6000, an orchestra of 100 harps, and the Band of the Welsh Guards.

In the early 1990s Songs of Praise was watched by nearly a quarter of the British population. In 1998 that had dropped to between 5 and 6 million and currently attracts not as many, but still millions of viewers each week.

Now I realise that *Songs of Praise* is not every one's cup of tea. Indeed a vicar writing in the Radio Times roundly criticised the programme.

Perhaps she was voicing the opinion of many Christians that it is not a substitute for belonging to a church. Nonetheless its facts and figures are pretty impressive. People who tell us that religion in this country is almost dead may well struggle to explain this *Songs of Praise* phenomenon. Why is this programme so popular? Why do people still like to sing hymns? Why are new hymns and songs churned out so prolifically? (Probably topping the production of *pop songs*.)

There is a broader question for us to answer which is this. Even if TV's *Songs of Praise* were to end next week, why would Christians, across the country and around the world, in churches large and small, still be found week by week singing their hymns and songs of praise? Why, in fact, do Christians sing at all? And why do they sing so much? "Methodism was born in song" begins the preface to the old Methodist Hymn Book. Why did John Wesley write those words? WHY DO CHRISTIANS SING?

Well, let's think about that. I'm suggesting three reasons, three words actually – all beginning with the letter H. The first word is HERITAGE. We sing because we have a heritage of singing and it's a heritage which goes back a long, long way.

Earlier in the service we sang the words: "Songs of praise the angels sang, Heaven with alleluias rang, When Jehovah's work begun, When God spoke and it was done." – referring to the creation, and you can't get any farther back than that. The suggestion that the world began with singing comes from the book of Job.

In chapter 38 God speaks to the unhappy, complaining sufferer: "Where were *you*," he asks, "when I laid the earth's foundations...when the morning stars sang together, and all the angels of God shouted for joy?"

This idea was taken up by the writer C.S.Lewis in one of his children's books. In *The Magician's Nephew* he describes the creation of the imaginary world of Narnia – a magic world which will be inhabited by talking animals but which will come under the rule of a wicked Queen, before a magnificent lion called Aslan comes to the rescue.

We read about all that in *The Lion, the Witch and the Wardrobe* which is the second of the seven chronicles of Narnia, but the whole saga begins with *The Magician's Nephew* and London in Victorian England when Sherlock Holmes lived in Baker Street and before cars replaced cabs pulled by horses. The scene is this: two children, their uncle, a cab driver and his horse have stumbled from our world into the darkness which is about to become the land of Narnia. They have been taken right back to the very beginning – the creation, the Genesis of Narnia. They arrived into a state of pitch black nothingness. They could not see anything and all they could hear were their own voices.

"Hush!" said the cabby. They all listened. In the darkness something was happening. A voice had begun to sing. It was very far away and Digory found it hard to decide from where it was coming. Sometimes it seemed to come from all directions at once. Sometimes he almost thought it was coming from beneath them, though they couldn't see the ground on which they stood. The voice continued to sing, giving encouragement for millions of stars to fill the heavens. They too were singing. Gradually the sky grew pale, changing from grey to white, to pink, to glorious gold, as with a mighty song the sun rose.

The singer was Aslan, the majestic, gentle lion, who they could now see pacing to and fro across the empty land, now starting a new softer song, more lilting, a gentle, rippling music. The valley grew green with grass and the hills dark with heather. As the song continued so did the creation – trees, streams, flowers, and then animals.

There was singing at the Creation suggests the writer of the ancient tale of Job and here it is endorsed by C.S. Lewis in lovely, poetic metaphor. We *know* that neither account is scientific but somehow or other it adds to our sense of wonder and worship as we grow in our appreciation that the "Hand that made us (and all things) is Divine." We really do live in a universe full of miracles galore.

Not only at the Creation do we find singing, but the rest of the Hebrew scriptures, incorporated into our Old Testament, is saturated in song and permeated with praise. And it's not just in the Psalms, (where you would expect it to be of course.) There is an interesting verse in the First Book of Chronicles (25v.6) which tells us that "God had given Heman 14 sons and 3 daughters and they all served under their father for the singing of the House of the Lord" – in other words the

Temple choir and orchestra which numbered (we are told) 288. 14 sons and 3 daughters! That is one way to keep up your choir and instrumentalist numbers!

Heman perhaps ought to be pronounced He Man! What would you call his wife, I wonder?

The New Testament continues the singing. We sang: "Songs of praise awoke the morn when the Prince of Peace was born." That makes us recall the Christmas reading where the shepherds are confronted by the message of the Angel and startled when suddenly with the angel there was a great company of the heavenly host praising God.

In the book of Acts and in the letters which follow we detect that the Early Church had a joy which made them sing and praise God. They just couldn't help it. So we find Paul and Silas in prison at Philippi, in an underground jail, shackled in chains, fastened in stocks, smarting from a beating. At the darkest hour of midnight what are they doing? Singing praises to God!

Oh and after the New Testament the singing doesn't stop. Rather the opposite. It seems to grow in volume and variety as an essential ingredient of Christian worship. These Christians: you just cannot stop them singing. They have even taken on a remarkable television series whose title describes what they sing – *Songs of Praise.*

Up in St Hilda's Monastery at Whitby in the 7th century a young cowherd called Caedmon could not sing a note. Miserably he had to leave the hall after supper when the monks sang their songs round the warm log fire. Outside in the cattle shed on his bed of straw Caedmon sleeps, and dreams. A voice comes to him, "Caedmon, sing to me." "I cannot sing. That's why I left the hall." "Caedmon, you *shall* sing!"

And Caedmon does sing. He turns Bible stories into sweet songs and sings them in the church, in the hall, in towns and villages, not in Latin but in the people's own language. Caedmon's songs were learned and sung by others, and loved.

Eleven centuries later came the great evangelical revival when "Methodism was born in song." The remarkable Wesley brothers – John the powerful preacher and Charles the prolific hymn writer with a mere six thousand of them!

Why do Christians sing? Because we have a glorious heritage of song. But that's not the only reason. Very briefly I make two other suggestions. We sing because we are happy and we sing because of Him – Jesus, who is our Lord and the Lord of the Church.

One of Charles Wesley's hymns *(My God I am thine)* has these words: "What a blessing to know that my Jesus is mine! In the heavenly Lamb Thrice happy I am, And my heart it doth dance at the sound of His name."

Jesus makes us happy, yes! But please note what the hymn spells out: not just happy or doubly happy even, but three times is the measure of happiness for those who have come to love and follow Jesus. Why even the mention of his name makes our heart leap and dance.

Of course when Christians talk about happiness we are not equating that with the frothy happiness presented by the media – a state which seems to depend on having money, achieving success in our careers and in our relationships, being well dressed, beautiful, fit and healthy. There's more to happiness than all those, important though they are. Perhaps a better word would be JOY, like that stillness at the bottom of the sea when storms may be raging at the surface. This is the deep down joy which enabled Paul and Silas to sing praises in their underground prison cell at midnight. This happiness or joy is a gift of faith, requiring our commitment to Jesus, and our response to his love for us: that love which is supremely demonstrated on a cross. It is Jesus who puts a song into our hearts.

Why do Christians sing? We sing because we have a heritage of song. We sing because we are happy in Jesus but underlying those two reasons we just sing because of Him.

Even if you could never join a choir because you cannot find a pitch or hold a note; even if you can only croak and your singing is an unmelodious pain it will still be recognised as a "joyful noise, to the Lord." When all is said and done, or sung, it is after all our *lives* which proclaim his power and perpetuate his praise. We can *all* (no exceptions) follow Paul's advice to the Christians at Colossae:

"Make melody *in your hearts* to the Lord by doing everything in the name of the Lord Jesus and by giving thanks to God the Father through Him."

May the life of our church and *your* life in the week ahead be saturated in song and permeated with praise. Amen

(Preached in the Leeds West Circuit in October and November 2014 at Wesley Road Chapel and Cookridge and Meanwood Methodist churches)

CAUGHT IN THE ACT

"Do not judge others," said Jesus, "so that God will not judge you" – or if you prefer The Message version: "Don't pick on people, jump on their failures, criticise their faults – unless, of course, you want the same treatment. That critical spirit has a way of boomeranging."

It seems to be the norm these days for people to be very harsh, destructive even, in their criticism of others. The media sets the bad example, may even have started the trend but certainly fuels it.

Take television's hospital dramas, for instance, where many patients are rude, aggressive and too demanding of medical staff.

Then there's Ann Robinson: 'Goodbye, you are the weakest link.' Alan Sugar: 'You're fired!' The "Let's Dance" panel: 'You move like a sack of potatoes.'

The so called "reality" shows such as "Big Brother" (and they're not true to real life are they?) rely on the public humiliation of participants in order to provide entertainment.

We could go on with the television, and we haven't even mentioned newspapers and magazines.

'Sticks and stones will break my bones but calling will not hurt me' we used to chant in the playground.

Don't you believe it!' Cruel words can be much more harmful than a punch on the nose. And such hurting can last a long, long time. How many adults still remember some of the unkind playground nicknames, or unhelpful comments on their school reports?

Jesus was sometimes blunt in his advice 'Go and sin no more', for instance. But he was rarely confrontational and never destructive.

Mostly he waited for folk to approach him. He didn't set out to find them and then assassinate their character. He would not refer to anybody as 'the weakest link,' not even Judas Iscariot.

Some who met Jesus came away feeling chastened, but there was always a positive intention and after the initial 'put down', further thought could lead them to ponder: 'Was Jesus right about me? Do I need to make adjustments to my life?'

Such thinking is the first step in what Christians call 'repentance'. Repentance is much more than being sorry. It's a sorrow which leads to changes in our ways of thinking and living.

Modern trends in judgment, fostered by parts of the media, do not leave a door open for sorrow and amendment.

If God treated us in the way in which they, and we, sometimes treat others where would we stand?

"Do not judge others, so that God will not judge you," Jesus says.

How such words pull us up sharp because we are all, without exception, guilty of occasionally having a go at others.

Our targets could include such as immigrants, gypsies, street beggars, drug addicts, binge drinkers, people we don't get on with, maybe even our neighbours, maybe even fellow worshippers!

For those seen as the worst offenders: "Lock them up and throw away the key!" certain newspapers would headline, using expressions like "They're a waste of space."

Hopefully Christians don't go as far as that – though the Psalms, which are part of our devotions, often do.

Do we not, though, sometimes find ourselves beginning to tread on that dangerous judgmental path where little or no mercy is shown?

Now, of course, we have to make judgments about people. Every time we vote in an election we decide who is worthy of our vote – because we trust them, We don't hire tradesman to do a job for us if we judge that they are not up to scratch. On a more personal level we make judgments about who we want to be our close friends and who to keep at arm's length.

Jesus wasn't saying "Never judge," in that sense and when, a few sentences later, he says, "Hypocrite! Take the beam out of your own eye before you remove the splinter from your neighbour's eye." we get the point. It is hypocrisy which Jesus condemns – - the tendency to express harsh criticism of others when deep within us there could be a streak of the same fault – even though to a much lesser degree and largely kept in control. Friend of John Wesley, the popular preacher George Whitefield, seeing a criminal on the way to the gallows, made his famous comment:

"There, but for the grace of God, go I." – a sentiment worth keeping in mind when we are tempted to voice derogatory opinions. Sometimes we would do well to just keep our mouths shut.

Jesus is the example to try to follow. He didn't use unkind words. He never wrote anyone off as worthless. He always saw the possibilities in people – no matter how much of a failure they appeared to be. Jesus even touched the lepers who were avoided by everyone else. He dined with despicable tax collectors and he allowed a woman with a doubtful reputation to anoint his feet with oil.

One of the legendary stories about Jesus tells of how he and his disciples saw a dog lying in the gutter. One by one the disciples condemned the dog: "What a mangy creature. It smells. It's full of fleas."

Jesus bent down and touched the unfortunate animal. "But see what beautiful eyes it has," he said.

In a children's address I hold up a large piece of white paper with a small smudge in the middle. "What is the first thing you see?" I ask. Invariably the answer is, "A dirty mark," rather than a big sheet of white paper.

I guess we all have the tendency to focus on the tiny faults in people rather than the much greater areas of good.

Looking for the best in people was what Jesus practised – and, thankfully, still does – with us. No matter how long ago, or how recently, we first embraced Christ and his teaching, no matter how many years we have been coming to church, or how often, we all have much to learn about grace and forgiveness , and gratitude and discipleship.

Let's think about how grateful we should be to Jesus as we sing the hymn Amazing Grace"

Caught in the act

There are lots of accounts in the Gospels of how Jesus welcomed individuals who had made a mess of the lives, or who were simply feeling bad about themselves. We learn how Jesus made them face up to their mistakes, offering them God's forgiveness, restoring their belief in themselves by pointing them in a new direction.

One such person was a woman accused of adultery. Let's remind ourselves of what happened.

Reading – John 8 v2-11

In today's society many people would not regard adultery as a terrible sin. Excuses are made, especially for those who "play away from home" Adultery is often glamourised on the telly. Portrayed as exciting, its consequences on family and friends are largely ignored and a blind eye is turned to all the heartbreak, anger and distress that marital infidelity inevitably brings.

In Jesus's day adultery was very much frowned upon. In a religious society the ancient Law of Moses, (interpreted as the Word of God himself), was regarded as sacrosanct.

A woman found guilty of adultery was subject to a death sentence – as was a man, though in this incident we have to ask, 'Where was the man?' Why didn't the Pharisees bring *him* to Jesus as well? As usual women bore the brunt of the blame. Religion always has had a habit of treating women as inferior to men. The Church became quite skilled at the practice, and to our shame, the attitude still exists in certain areas.

I sometimes joke that the Church will not really have arrived until we have a black female lesbian as the Pope – but it's not just the Roman Catholic Church is it, which has been reluctant to take equality on board? We have all been guilty over the years.

It is interesting that this gospel story does not appear in any of the great manuscripts of the New Testament. Questions arise such as, "Did it actually happen?" And if so, was it deliberately suppressed by the early church in order to avoid scandal because Jesus could be seen here as taking too lenient a view on such a serious sin? Scholars still debate such issues.

I guess this story is not much preached on either because it has no slot in our fixed Church Lectionary. So what are we to make of this incident?

I suggest that there are three human elements here. Firstly we see how the Pharisees issue a stern challenge. Then how Jesus offers a second chance And finally how the woman has a simple choice.

A stern challenge, a second chance and a simple choice.

We have to remember that the Scribes and the Pharisees who brought this woman to Jesus were the religious leaders of the day. They were the upholders of morals and the pillars of society.

In Jesus they perceived not only a challenge to their authority and standing but also a threat to the nation's religion of which they were God's guardians.

So they were on the lookout for an opportunity to put this dangerous man, Jesus, in his place. Here, in this woman, was their chance to discredit their opponent.

"Teacher," they said with feigned homage, "this woman was caught in the act of adultery. The Law of Moses prescribes death by stoning. What do you say about her?"

A very clever question! They thought they had Jesus trapped.

If he recommended mercy then he would be undermining God's Laws as well as appearing to give approval to what was regarded as the third gravest sin, following idolatry and murder. On the other hand, if Jesus recommended death he would lose the reputation he had gained for love and mercy, and people would no longer call him 'Friend of Sinners.'

Anyway, only the Romans could order death, and if Jesus did so he would be seen as a criminal, taking the law into his own hands.

It was a stern challenge those religious leaders gave to Jesus and when he stooped down to write with his finger in the sand they thought they had him trapped, that he didn't know how to reply, that he was ignoring the question and hoping they would go away.

There has been much speculation about what Jesus wrote on the ground. Was he just doodling – giving himself time to pray and to work out how to answer? Was he averting his eyes in shame and pity at the anger, lust and cruelty confronting him? Was he writing down their sins so they would come and read them and have to face up to their own shortcomings?

We're not told. But for me the picture of Jesus's actions here is of one who is calm and in control, not one who is defeated. I wondered whether to use the word 'strong' or 'stern' to describe the challenge of the Pharisees. Stern seems better because stern, harsh attitudes are a danger for all who embrace religious zeal.

"There's a wideness in God's mercy like the wideness of the sea," proclaimed Frederick Faber in the opening line of his hymn. But he also gives a warning in a later verse: "But we make his love too narrow By false limits of our own; And we magnify his strictness With a zeal he will not own."

Religious zeal can lead us to the opinion that we understand God – that he has chosen us to be his moral agents.

It can make us ready to condemn the sins of society without trying to understand why people behave badly. It can lead us to intolerance of others.

Religious zeal has bred slavery, apartheid, narrow denominationalism, suicide bombings, hellfire preaching the taunting of those whose beliefs on abortion or the rights of the gay community seem at odds with a fundamentalist interpretation of scripture. Beware of this sort of religious zeal. Such fervour, it seems to me, runs counter to the image of Jesus which this story presents.

For against the sternness of the Pharisees' challenge is set the second chance which Jesus gave to this unfortunate woman who was being used as a pawn in their underhand game.

The Pharisees issued a stern challenge whereas Jesus offered a second chance. The Pharisees wished to condemn, Jesus wanted to forgive.

He always does – and when we look into our own lives we can thank God that the door to his mercy is never closed to us.

Jesus said to the woman, and he says to us, something like this: "Look, I know you've made a mess of things, but life is not finished yet. I am giving you another chance- the chance to redeem yourself, or rather, the chance to let me redeem you.

In his commentary on this passage in John's Gospel William Barclay quoted these words from a poem: "How I wish that there was some wonderful place Called the Land of Beginning Again, Where all our mistakes and all our heartaches And all our poor selfish grief Could be dropped like a shabby old coat at the door, And never put on again."

Well, in Jesus there *is* such a place, for his is the Gospel of the Second Chance. No matter who we are, no matter what we have done, in Jesus we can begin again: "Ransomed, healed, restored, forgiven."

Jesus showed this woman – and he shows us – that he is interested not only in what we have been, but more so in what, with his help, we can become.

The story is told of a young clergyman, appointed to the post of Prison Chaplain, being taken to meet an assembly of prisoners.

As he was lead to the platform he felt all eyes fixed on him and wondered desperately what he could say to these men.

Unfortunately he tripped over the top step and fell flat on his face. The audience erupted in laughter.

He picked himself up, dusted himself down and when the noise had died away he addressed them: "I have only one thing to say to you and it's this: When a man falls in life he needn't stay down. He can get up and start again."

Every act of worship, every encounter with God, (however that may happen) is an invitation for us to get up and begin again - and to go on our way rejoicing in the knowledge that "No condemnation now I dread, Jesus, and all in him, is mine."

Jesus offers us a second chance, yes and a third, a fourth, a fifth, ad infinitum.

Do not imagine though that here is an invitation to go on sinning wilfully again and again, as our third point hopefully will make clear.

Having been offered a second chance the woman now has a simple choice.

"Go, and sin no more," Jesus told her. He didn't say, "Your life is OK. Just carry on living in the same way."

No. He said something like this: "Your life, as it is, is wrong. You need to change it. You need to stop this sin, this adultery which is bringing unhappiness to you and to others."

We can see then that here is no cheap grace being offered, no easy forgiveness.

If we embrace the love of Jesus and invite him into our lives he confronts the badness in us with the goodness in him, and we know we have to change. We don't do it by ourselves. It's a partnership of trust – and there will be setbacks. We shall never achieve perfection in this life.

Maybe that is our ultimate goal. Charles Wesley thought so when he indicated that the Christian pilgrimage is a matter of "being changed from glory into glory, till in heaven we take our place."

But that may be a long way off for us (we hope!). In the meantime we each have a simple choice, and we can make it every morning by praying: "Lord Jesus, today I'm going to follow you."

We don't know what happened subsequently to this woman but in that potentially life saving encounter with Jesus she was offered the simple choice – to go back to her old ways or to start out on a new way.

The Pharisees wrote her off as a miserable sinner and I guess she felt rotten about herself as well as scared stiff of the consequences.

Jesus showed her that she might think of herself as a miserable sinner, but in his eyes she was a potential saint.

How do you see yourself – miserable sinner or potential saint? It's a simple choice. Regardless of how low we may be feeling about our lives just now, let us each say to ourselves as we leave church this morning:

"Jesus tells me I'm a forgiven sinner and therefore a potential saint."

You, who are saints in the making, keep on saying that and keep on believing it: for, as the story of this woman tells us, Jesus offers us the Gospel of the Second Chance.

Forgiven sinners, potential saints! No wonder we can sing, and tell others of God's amazing love.

"Amazing love! How can it be that thou my God shouldst die for me?"

(Preached at Cookridge Methodist Church, Leeds October 13th 2013)

LESSONS LEARNED FROM NATIONAL SERVICE

The following is an extract from my inaugural address to the Leeds District Methodist Men's Luncheon Club when I was inducted as their Annual President on Wednesday 19th September, 2012.

When I die… and isn't that a cheerful way in which to begin my year of office as President of the prestigious Leeds District Methodist Men's Luncheon Club? Our title is quite a mouthful is it not?

When I die, if a post mortem is performed, they will probably find two numbers engraved on my heart. The first one is my mother's Co-op number! The other I was given by the army. It is seared into the memories of all who were called upon to give service to King or Queen and country. From time to time the suggestion gets floated: "Let's reintroduce National Service It will help to reduce unemployment for the young, it will keep them off the streets causing trouble and it will instil into them a sense of discipline and respect." Well it just wouldn't work would it, for lots of reasons.

Some of those who went through a period of National Service may think that it was a waste of two years but I guess that a few of us took from it at least some useful lessons which we have developed as the years have gone by. Let me share with you a handful of the ways in which my time of conscription planted seeds which have help to shape the sort of person I have become. "Lessons learned from National Service."

I have three headings (you can tell I'm a preacher). The first one is LEARNING HOW TO STAND ON YOUR OWN FEET.

On the 1st July 1954 I, very unwillingly, became a soldier in the Royal Engineers and was shunted off to Malvern in Worcestershire for basic training – "square bashing" as it was called. This followed a medical in which I tried to press down from the knees to create flat feet, and coughed occasionally. It was to no avail. It seemed that if you could breathe and stand up you were bound to be passed as A1.

After all the rigours and traumas of basic training and a brief leave I was shipped off to the Canal Zone in Egypt for 12 months and from there it was on to Cyprus, where Archbishop Makarios, General Grivas and the EOKA resistance movement were beginning to cause trouble. Eight months were spent in Cyprus on what became Active Service before I was demobbed in late June 1956 arriving back with a really deep suntan to enjoy going swimming with the girls at church.

The is one thing I definitely picked up from those army days, some might call it a foible. I don't think it's an obsession, but it can sometimes be a nuisance. It is my admiration for tidiness, neatness, things done in an orderly fashion. I guess such standards were drilled into us in basic training. I remember those daily morning inspections. "Stand by your beds!" was the order and we jumped to it, rigidly at attention, eyes fixed forward, waiting nervously for the officer and sergeant major to pass by and praying that they would find nothing to criticise. Our beds were neatly made, our blankets and sheets had been carefully folded – blanket, sheet, blanket, sheet – all boxed up within a surrounding blanket. There were perhaps twenty trainee soldiers (in the Royal Engineers we were sappers, not privates) in each hut. We stood in two rows down the sides of the hut facing each other across the highly polished floor in the middle – a sort of sacred space which we all tried to avoid walking across. Everything had to be lined up dead straight for those inspections – beds, blankets, kit laid out on the beds, including our bulled up polished boots with the correct number of studs in the soles and our evenly blancoed belts with their gleaming brassoed badges. Hours and hours were spent achieving the mirror like appearance of our boot toecaps. The process involved dusters, black polish, water, a spoon which we heated over a candle as we laboriously built up a veneer of polish.

All of this neatness and order maybe explains why, when I go into church on Sunday mornings, I look to see if the communion table is exactly centred beneath the Cross on the front wall, whether the chairs have been lined up properly, and is the hymn board cockeyed? Oh and the hymn books! Quite often they have just been put haphazardly on the little shelves beneath each seat. I want to tidy them and sometimes do if I'm in the building on my own. Hymns and Psalms on the left side, Songs of Fellowship on the right, on each end chair a Bible in the middle of the shelf. Then I can stand at the back of the church, like a sergeant major in the barrack room, and think "Yes! That looks good! Nothing higgledy-piggledy here! Everything in perfect order!"

In one of her household books Mrs Beeton used the saying, "A place for everything and everything in its place." Not a bad motto to have and I read somewhere that Susannah Wesley must have had a similar rule for her large family. But my leaning in that direction can be a nuisance. I blame the army – not just the basic training because in Egypt we swept the sand round our tents into neat, parallel and evenly spaced lines and in Cyprus I was once put on a charge for not removing the sheets from beneath the blanket on an otherwise perfectly made bed. I was on escort duty that morning which involved getting up at 4 o'clock. The inspection took place before I got back!

All the military training is to get you to respond to orders, without question – a bit like one of Pavlov's dogs. It seems to work, but not entirely. For instance I found myself asking, "What is the point of cutting grass on a sunny Sunday afternoon, with a penknife? I could never see the point of my daily morning job, before the inspection, of polishing the dustbin or of brassoing the urinals, of having to remove the plastic buttons from our greatcoats and sewing on brass ones (something else to polish), and I couldn't for the life of me when on bayonet practice visualise the suspended stuffed sack as a Korean Communist. To me it remained a sack.

Years later though, when I was married, I always polished the children's shoes before I went to bed and laid the table for breakfast. Crazy really but a set of standards had been drilled into me. When I became a teacher I always wore a suit at school (not many of my colleagues did) and I still don't feel dressed properly without a tie. So I shudder a bit when I see interviews on the TV news where men appear with stubbly chins and jeans and crumpled shirts looking as if they have just got out of bed and haven't even washed. Scruffy! But I'm old fashioned and I'm army trained!

Standards, personal pride, a sense of orderliness, discipline: all that comes into one general lesson learned from National Service. Within that wide area there are lots of "household" skills such as learning how to sew, how to iron, how to darn socks (thankfully a now redundant art), keeping yourself and surroundings tidy and, overall, learning how to stand on your own feet.

You cannot stand on your own feet without the help of friends along your way. That brings me to the second lesson learned from those two years which were snatched from a young man's life in those far off days. That lesson is this – LEARNING TO VALUE THE IMPORTANCE OF FRIENDS.

Friends in the Army are particularly important. That is made clear when we see funerals on television of young men tragically killed in Afghanistan, in the tributes paid to them by their mates and their officers. You could not manage in the armed forces without friends that you really know and really trust. Away from your families, and in all the new and scary situations, you develop a few close friendships and you "muck in" together to battle your way through – hence the army slang word "mucker."

We all had our muckers. We lived cheek by jowl,we shared our thoughts and our ideas, our sorrows and our joys. When they left for demob we were bereft for a while. We kept in contact with a few and nearly sixty years later I still exchange Christmas letters with two of my muckers who are still alive. I have come to see the truth of that verse from Proverbs which says that "A friend sticks closer than a brother" and also to contemplate that when we talk about Jesus and his disciples we could refer to them as "Jesus and his Muckers"!

Let me mention some of my army muckers. There was Peter Hopkins who became the Best Man at our wedding, whom I reckon was literally the best man I have ever known. Peter would do anything for anybody, no matter how inconvenient – and always with a smile. He seemed to be on the lookout for people to help. Peter and his wife Margaret had four children and Patricia and I had three and we all spent some wonderful holidays together in the remote village of Marloes on the lovely Pembrokeshire coast. Sadly Peter died at the age of 33 but our two families have stayed very close in the years since.

Then there was Rhys Thomas. With a name like that, Rhys obviously had Welsh roots but actually came from Watford. He became a Baptist minister in

Bristol and we went to his wedding there. Rhys now lives in Frinton on Sea and is active in his local church especially as a pastoral visitor.

Robin McGlashan won boxing blues at both Oxford and Cambridge Universities. Robin became an Anglican priest who went to India as a missionary and taught New Testament Greek at Tirunavelli Theological Seminary.

I will never forget our Free Church Padre in Cyprus, RAF Squadron Leader Rev John Murrie from the Church of Scotland, who had a real sense of fun and mischief. Possessor of a loud infectious laugh his voice boomed out above the congregation when we sang the hymns – especially during "From sinking sands he lifted me." I could imagine him standing on his seat to sing those words. Surprisingly he never did.

Also there was John Mankey. I never knew John all that well but I admired his quiet and humble Christian ways and John, who was to become an Anglican vicar in Australia, was, maybe unknowingly to him, instrumental in my own deeper personal commitment to Christ. I'll tell you in a minute how that happened but I just want to underline that a major lesson learned from National Service (for me) was to appreciate the value of friends.

Friends played a vital part in what I consider to be the third and final lesson learned. I call this STEPS IN FAITH. We all learn a lot from friends and writers, preachers and leaders and just ordinary people within the family of the Church. Sometimes it's just a broader knowledge of the workings of the Church that we pick up, but often we are learning what being a follower of Jesus involves such as lessons in prayer and reading the scriptures, ventures in service and witness, how we can become wiser, more humble, more obedient Christians. All this we learn from Christian friends, which is why those who say "I can be a Christian without going to church" are missing a large part of the plot.

When I arrived in Egypt, at Fayid in the Canal Zone, my first impressions were, "What a God forsaken place this is!" In a giant con trick we had been given the choice of where we would like to be posted. The first choice for most was The British Isles (regular periods of home leave were given). Second choice was Germany (a leave every six months). Third came the Far East (if you were going overseas for 20 months it might as well be somewhere exciting and exotic.) The last on everybody's list was Egypt. Nobody wanted to be posted to Egypt!

So here I was in a land full of sand, and flies and heat and barbed wire and more flies. You could recognise someone who had served in Egypt (it was said) because they acquired the habit of flicking away flies. After today's lovely dinner I will not go into details of our camp toilet facilities! Along one side of the camp was the Sweet Water Canal, and there's a misnomer. Among the general detritus floating on the water I recall once seeing a dead donkey.

How is it then that, given this situation, I was able to write on the fly leaf of a Chain Reference Bible I purchased some months later whilst on leave in Jerusalem, this verse from Deuteronomy:

"Thou shalt remember that thou wast a bondman (a slave) in the land of Egypt and the Lord thy God redeemed thee." (15v.15)

Egypt hadn't changed but I had. In Egypt God became very real to me. In Egypt I found God, or more accurately, God found me. It happened largely through the fellowship of the Mission to Mediterranean Garrisons or the MMG as we called it. The MMG was open to service personnel of all ranks and any denomination. You could go there to get away from the camps, to relax, to play games, to attend meetings if you wanted to. Three ladies ran the MMG at Fayid. I used to go to their sit down Sunday lunch. It was like a touch of home.Every Wednesday evening we combined forces and travelled to another MMG farther south to a Gospel Meeting. We listened to testimonies, sang rousing choruses and hymns, heard an address from an invited speaker. Often there would be an appeal and invariably lives were given to Christ. It was all very inspiring and I remember one night in late November 1954, as our open army lorry took us back to Fayid, gazing up at the beautiful, star filled Egyptian night sky, praising God and singing my own hallelujahs. Life wasn't so bad after all.

The following evening I went to a prayer meeting organised by John Mankey. Very few were there, perhaps half a dozen or so. John's prayers moved me. They were in the vein of David's Psalm of Confession:

"Have mercy upon me, O God, according to thy loving kindness… I acknowledge my transgressions and my sin is everbefore me… Create in me a clean heart, and renew a right spirit within me…..a broken and a contrite heart thou wiltnot despise." (Psalm 51)

I had not forgotten the hallelujahs of the previous evening but the moment for introspection had arrived, and new perspectives began to dawn. Before being called up I attended services and youth fellowships at Wesley Road Methodist Church in Armley. I taught in Sunday School and had been received into membership. I do not therefore refer to this as a conversion experience but it was a significant step in my faith journey.

It was at the MMG that I first ventured into preaching – a not very good sermon I have to say. That journey took another seven years before I qualified – and I'm still learning.

I also experienced the freedom and the joys of charismatic style worship. As a former choirboy I already appreciated the order and beauty of formal Anglican worship. My horizons during National Service were being opened to the rich variety of Christian worship styles.

I began too to recognise the relative unimportance of denominations, whilst still valuing the roots and heritages of our own particular traditions. On the troopship "Empire Ken", Egypt bound, a Bible Study had been arranged so I had gone along and was surprised to find that among our number was a Roman

Catholic. Way back in the early 1950's our church had no dealings with the Roman Catholics, whom we regarded with some suspicion. In Egypt and in Cyprus there were three churches on the camp – the Church of England, the Roman Catholic and the free Church, which embraced various denominations and at the MMG we were all in together. Denominations didn't matter.

I have been known occasionally to write to the Methodist Recorder. Recently they began a series called "Proud to be a Methodist". I found it to be disturbing so I sent a letter saying that whilst I didn't care for the word "Proud," I was nonetheless grateful for all that Methodism has given me and I gave a few examples. Then I used the word BUT and went on to mention some of the things within our church which do not actually fill me with pride. I also wrote that there was no way I could put up a poster at our now ecumenical church at Wesley Road saying "Proud to be a Methodist." That would be divisive. The whole campaign seemed to me to be out of step in this modern age of church unity. Surprisingly (or not!) my letter was not published or my suggestion that "Proud to be a Christian" would be a better title. That title would not offend people of different faiths – that other "Great Divide" which we are seeking to break down whenever Christians, Muslims, Hindus, Sikhs, Buddhists and the rest co-operate in the struggle against injustice, indifference to the God of all people, and the various ills and challenges confronting our society and the wider world.

One other important step in faith which I began to learn and appreciate all those years ago has to do with the importance of prayer. I guess I'm still a beginner. This was a lesson learned on Guard duty. An all-night guard duty of one sort or another came round about once every seven or eight days. Occasionally I found myself walking around the inside of the perimeter fence of the Middle East Headquarters where I worked during the day as a clerk in the Troop Movements section. The complex covered several acres. We were on duty from six in the evening to six next morning. Two two-hour sessions were spent guarding, the rest you tried to get some sleep. We drew lots to choose who went out on patrol first, (from 6 pm to 8 and then midnight to 2 am), who went second (8 till 10 and 2 to 4 am), and whose turn was the unlucky third (10 to midnight and 4 am to 6).

You were bound to be patrolling most of the time in the dark. But it was never really dark. In fact when there was a full moon you could almost read a newspaper. You didn't because the duty officer may have caught you. You were on your own and I whiled away my time thinking and praying. I can understand what attracted the early Desert Fathers to the peace and solitude of that sort of environment, especially at night time beneath a clear sky and so many stars, with the odd shooting one. Whenever I hear Psalm 8 I am taken back to those lonely, beautiful nights on guard.

"When I consider thy heavens, the work of thy fingers, the moon and the stars which thou hast ordained; what is man, that thou art mindful of him...?"

Nearly sixty years after all those events I have moved on in my thinking, my understanding of faith matters and certainly in my theology. The ethos at the MMG was charismatic and fundamentalist and I have become quite liberal and radical – but I owe a lot to their love and enthusiasm, and am thankful for that.

Lessons I learned from National Service then: How to stand on my own feet; The importance of friends; How we must always be trying to move forward in the faith, always open to learning new lessons.

Feet, friends, faith. A final F is the word FINISH. That's what I am now doing. Thank you for listening, for stifling your yawns especially after a good lunch, and for not pretending to play your violins which is what my children do whenever I am tempted to talk about National Service!

PRAYING FOR
PRESIDENT PUTIN

A problem confronts and disturbs me. It is a faith problem so I turn to you, my sisters and brothers in Christ, for help and advice, following the instructions of St Paul that we should share one another's burdens. (Galatians 6v2)

I am not wrestling with beliefs: my trust in God's love for me actually grows stronger as I get older. I am not finding prayer impossible, or going to church. Sharing God's love, being kind to others and being concerned for their wellbeing are not always easy but they remain, as an inviting challenge.

All would seem reasonably well (you might conclude). There is though one area of my prayer life wherein my problems arise, especially when I am leading prayer on behalf of others – in public prayers as opposed to private intercessions. I have to admit that praying for President Vladimir Putin, in public prayers particularly, is not easy. Maybe some of you can point me in the right direction?

Do you remember the long period of the "Irish Troubles." Service after service I prayed from the pulpit for peace in Ireland. (And in my own prayers I would be asking God to bang a few heads together.)

Forward to present times and the Russian crisis. I never envisaged suggesting to God that any person should be removed from the scene (perhaps by his own supporters) but I have to admit that Mary's words in Luke's Magnificat have their appeal: "Lord, bring down the mighty from their seat." With Putin in mind I can say "Amen" to that plea. But in doing so, how far am I straying from the command to "Love your enemies"?

Love your enemies, Jesus told his disciples, pray for those who despitefully use you, forgive-even to the point of pushing yourself into a pacifist stance. I get all that and I take it on board, at the same time seeing apparent inconsistencies between the reported words of Jesus and his actions. For instance, how far is taking up a whip to clear the traders and money changers from the Temple courts an act of love and how could he call Herod a fox – a killer of innocent creatures? New Testament scholars have tried to explain all this in terms of righteous anger; but what exactly *is* righteous anger?

"Turn the other cheek" we read in the Sermon on the Mount so that's one avenue worth exploring when we are confronted with the challenge of how to deal with spiteful attacks on us. At the ultimate extreme of course the prayer of Jesus from the cross "Father forgive them. They do not realise what they are doing," is there to strengthen us. We pray that we shall never find ourselves in such a dire situation.

Recently in a TV interview a refugee with her child said that the only way this will end was when Putin dies. There is a lot of hatred for the man. The daily news gives us the information and so feeds that. As a Christian and as a preacher I felt the need to dig deeper. In researching the problem I turned to our scriptures for clues. I found that some of the Psalms are filled with reactions to hatred, from ordinary people like us. The Message Version captures well our own feelings (though we must remember that here is one man's paraphrase of the scriptures and it has not the authority and scholarship of the many widely accepted versions of the Bible.)

Here are some words from Psalm 56 in The Message:

"Take my side, God – I'm getting kicked around, stomped on every day. Not a day goes by but somebody beats me up.....Pay them back. Get angry God! Down with these people!.... If my enemies run away...then I'll know that God is on my side....I trust in God. What can mere mortals do to me?"

The next four Psalms are in similar vein. I would not advise any preacher, (including me), to choose the first verse of Psalm 58 as the text for their sermon:

"Is this any way to run a country?" But forgive me, I digress.

My research of the scriptures has presented some interesting questions which I would like to share with you before closing.

In John's Gospel chapter 11 verses 49 to 50 we read;

"Caiaphas the High Priest said to the Council it is better for you to have one man die for the people than to have the whole nation destroyed. He did not say this on his own but being High Priest he prophesied that Jesus was about to die for the nation... From that day on they planned to put him to death."

It seems odd that Caiaphas the arch enemy of Jesus should, according to this early Christian scripture, become part of the divine plan. It reminds me of how the Prophet Isaiah has God describing the Babylonian Emperor (an ancient President Putin-like leader) described by God through the words of Isaiah as "my anointed, my servant – although you do not acknowledge me."(45v4-5). We have to admire such faith which can see in disaster evidence of God's love and give him credit for outcomes that are good.

What is the prophet saying, what are the compilers of scripture saying, what is God's message? Surely not that God's enemies such as Caiaphas and Cyrus have become his friends and servants?

Perhaps we are to understand that, no matter how evil people can be and how bad a situation has become, ultimately God will always have our interests at heart: "All things work together for good for those who love God" as St Paul wrote (Romans 8v28).

Is this the kind of resolve which has produced the indomitable courage and strength shown by Ukranian soldiers and civilians? "With Christ within the fight we'll win on the victory side," the old chorus goes.

It's all a bit puzzling isn't it and it does not take away my problem of how as a preacher I can cope with Vladimir Putin in my public prayers.

If Putin is a problem for me how much more is he a problem for God? We proclaim God's loving forgiveness but must not justice have to be part of the process? The daily catalogue of unspeakable atrocities carried out in Putin's name will rightly result in a United Nations trial, we surmise. Such an outcome is no cause for gloating though. Sorrow is more appropriate – that we have allowed the world to become so disjointed. So, brothers and sisters in Christ, my appeal for help remains.

Finally the thought occurs to me, and maybe to you, does what you have just heard or read qualify as a sermon anyway? Or is it just a discussion document from a confused.com preacher?

And that is a further topic for consideration!

(Written in April 2022. Shared with a couple of others but not preached)